LORDS OF THE SCAFFOLD

Geoffrey Abbott served in the RAF until 1974, when he left to become a member of the Body of Yeomen Warders at the Tower of London. The visiting public's obsession with the subject of executioners prompted him to write *Lords of the Scaffold*. He is also the author of books about ghosts, beefeaters, the Tower of London and the prisoners who escaped from there. He and his wife now live in the Lake District, where he enjoys writing, visiting castles and being Mace Bearer to the Mayor of Kendal.

Lords of the Scaffold

A History of Execution

Geoffrey Abbott

Yeoman Warder (rtd)
HM Tower of London
Member of Her Majesty's Bodyguard
of the Yeomen of the Guard Extraordinary

HEADLINE

First published in Great Britain in 1991
by Robert Hale Limited

First published in paperback in 1992
by HEADLINE BOOK PUBLISHING PLC

10 9 8 7 6 5 4 3 2 1

ISBN 0 7472 3879 0

Printed and bound in Great Britain by
HarperCollins Manufacturing, Glasgow

HEADLINE BOOK PUBLISHING PLC
Headline House
79 Great Titchfield Street
London W1P 7FN

Contents

Illustrations

Picture Credits

3: Hulton Picture Company; 5: Board of Trustees of the Royal Armouries

Prints provided by Kentdale Studio, Kendal

This book is dedicated to all those who were unjustly executed; the fault lies not with the executioners but with those who, chosen by the people, made the laws.

Acknowledgements

As befits the subject of this book, many heads got together in its execution! Among the more important owners of those vital appendages to whom thanks are hereby tendered, are the Officers of the Tower of London past and present, Yeoman Warder Brian Harrison, Assistant Curator of Armour Karen Watts and the Board of Trustees of the Royal Armouries; assistance from the staffs of the British Library and Guildhall Library, London, from Dorothy Atherston, Court Keeper of Lancaster Castle, Lancashire County Council and Calderdale Library, Halifax, Yorkshire, has been invaluable, as have the facilities afforded by the international staffs of the NATO libraries in Germany, Holland and France during the years 1956-1974.

Whilst every effort has been made to trace copyright to all material in this book, the author apologizes if he has inadvertently failed to credit any ownership of copyright.

Steal not this book, my honest friend
For fear the gallows be your end
And when you die the Lord will say
'Where is the book you stole away!'

popular verse, 1780

Introduction

Accounts of criminal trials published in old books and documents generally go into much detail of the court proceedings. The judge's name, the lawyers' speeches, evidence given by the witnesses, even the prisoners' protestations, are covered in full. And when executions were held in public, news sheets described each one minutely, dwelling avidly on the victim's behaviour, the crowd's reactions. Yet little if anything was said about the official presiding over the dreaded finale. He was referred to only as the 'executioner', thereby implying that he was unworthy of further identification, except as an object of scorn.

This deliberate omission was as unjust as it was undeserved. Executioners were no faceless, nameless pieces of the law's machinery, but were as necessary to society as were the public prosecutor, the lord chamberlain and indeed the prime minister of the day. As one political philosopher, on being presented with an abstract scenario for the perfect and ideal community commented wryly, *'Et qui videra les pôts de chambre?'* – but who will empty the chamber pots?

Executioners may not have been liked or likeable, but if the rule of law included the death penalty, society could not function without them. And while honours and praise were heaped on those who captured, prosecuted and passed sentence on the enemies of society, the men who carried out those sentences were at best shunned, at worst loathed and despised.

Yet they were individuals like anyone else of their day and age. Some bred rabbits, others had pet dogs. Some composed religious verse, others drew portraits of their 'clients'. Some wrote their autobiographies, others couldn't even sign their own name. Some wept before picking up the axe, others gloated as they positioned the noose. And while some died in their own beds, others swung on their own gallows or were beheaded by their guillotine.

They played a more decisive part in history than many a politician, for they dispatched kings and queens, priests and pirates, heretics and highwaymen. In Victor Hugo's *Mary Tudor* the author has Joshua say: 'Mind you, the man who knows the history of these times is the turnkey [warder] at the Tower of London.'

To which Simon Renard replies, 'You're mistaken, master, it's the executioner!'

And when the law demanded, they burned women and dismembered men. They were adept at wielding the whip and the branding iron, the thumbscrew and the slitting knife. If history were a tape recording, their voices would ring out from court and scaffold.

'A fair mark, my lord,' as they assured the judge of their skill with the branding iron.

'Behold the head of a traitor,' as they held the severed head high for public approval.

In the main they were impartial towards their victims. When backs were bared it mattered not whether the whip evoked feminine shrieks or masculine yells, and all necks were the same when the axe was poised, the noose adjusted or the guillotine blade released.

The executioner's role in society was reflected in some of the names applied to him: 'Finisher of the Law', 'Executioner General of Great Britain', 'Monsieur de Paris'. Others were less complimentary, ranging from 'Surveyor of the New Drop' and 'Apparator [Operator] of the Necklace' to 'Topman' and 'William Boilman', the last referring to that part of the English executioner's job which entailed the boiling of the dismembered limbs of traitors in order to preserve them when displayed as deterrents.

For hundreds of years public executions were major

attractions, attended by thousands of spectators. The star or stars of the show were of course the pitiable wretches who were to be executed, but it was the executioner himself who always played the strong supporting role, in more ways than one. He was the darling of the crowd if he put on a good performance or if the condemned man deserved to die, but a villain when he botched the execution or the felon happened to be a local hero.

Some were prominent because of those whom they dispatched, Brandon beheading Charles I, Bull executing Mary, Queen of Scots, Sanson decapitating Louis XVI. Some were infamous for their callous inaccuracy, Ketch needing five strokes with the axe to finish off James, Duke of Monmouth, the German Valtin Deusser requiring three blows with the sword to end the life of his female victim.

Humane executioners introduced improvements. Hangman Marwood devised the 'long drop' technique which ensured a speedier oblivion, Pierrepoint refined the preliminaries so that only twenty seconds elapsed between cell and drop, and the German Schmidt interceded on behalf of women guilty of infanticide, urging that they be hanged or beheaded rather than tied up in a sack and drowned.

The identities of many executioners were never publicized, either because it was considered unimportant, or to screen them from later reprisals. But whether their names are known or not, their victims certainly deserve a place in this book, whether they knelt upright for the sword, bent over the block or lay prone beneath the guillotine's blade.

The methods of dispatch also call for close study. In this day and age we tend to accept things as they are. We have television, radio, telephones, computers, devices so complex that we do not even start to consider how they work, but just take them for granted.

But that does not mean that we should stifle all curiosity, especially about the times when nearly everything was accomplished the hard way, by human hand and eye. Grinding corn, milking cows, making bread, just about every process of life was achieved manually and apparently successfully.

But how about the process of death? From many history

books we get the impression that it was all too easy. On the scaffold the blade descended, the criminal died, the crowd cheered, and justice was done. We naturally assume that the executioner just swung the axe or sword, or released the guillotine blade, and that was that. Job done, next please.

But pause to think. Better still, feel the back of your own neck – four, five inches in length? A small target indeed for the man standing over you, his knuckles white as he grips the axe, his nerves taut and twitching under the concentrated gaze of thousands of spectators. Will he sway off aim as you stare blindly down into the waiting basket? If he does, will you instinctively bring your hands up, only to have them amputated by his second strike?

Even if the judicial weapon isn't the brutal, unwieldy axe but the precisely balanced sword, can you guarantee to stay absolutely still as you kneel upright? Will his foot slip on the bloodied boards as he swings the heavy blade? And if you are the victim of the guillotine, is it as foolproof as they say, or could it jam, inches above your quivering neck? Will you really feel your severed head lifted high, your glazing eyes blinking at the crowd before your senses finally and irrevocably ebb away?

So much for the human element, but what about the execution instruments themselves? Their design and accuracy had to be evolved laboriously, long before high-carbon steel, metal-fatigue analysers or impact-testing equipment were developed. Everything was rough and ready. And why not, for after all, criminals had broken the law so why should they be entitled to a painless death? Society also had to decide how to extract the maximum amount of deterrence from the carrying out of the death sentence, how best to utilize the criminals' mortal remains in order to warn would-be wrongdoers.

No society's justice was perfect, no weapon infallible, no executioner unfailingly accurate. Axe blows went awry, swords swerved, guillotines seized, mishaps rarely evident from the bland statements of fact in the history books.

In the following pages the scaffold curtains will be

drawn back, to reveal to anyone who has ever swung a racket – and missed the ball; to anyone who, when slicing bread, has all but severed a finger; who, on closing a drawer, has managed to jam it immovable, half in, half out; that human errors which matter little in everyday life are catastrophic when they occur on the scaffold.

Across the world many methods of execution have been used, from guillotine to gas chamber, by axe or by arrows, swords or strangulation, drowning or dismembering. Men, women too, have been shot, garotted, hanged or burned to death, depending on their country and crime.

But whether death came by cold steel or hot lead, hempen rope or electric current, reading about other people's executions is never dull, as the following account shows. And if you have ever wondered what really happened to those severed heads, read on!

All these grim punishments were presided over by the executioner, the Lord of the Scaffold. You may not have liked him to be your neighbour, but his murderous victims would have been even more unacceptable. By his very actions he changed history – and who can state categorically that it was for the worse?

1 Aristocrats of the Axe

Although the last execution by the axe took place nearly 250 years ago, the implications are still part of our everyday vocabulary. 'You're for the chop!' we say, forecasting dire punishment, or 'You'll get it in the neck for this!'

And when, on conducting guided tours around the Tower of London, the author would facetiously misquote Henry VIII as saying 'Tails I win ...', the listening crowd, without any prompting, would instinctively finish off the saying, 'Heads you lose!', invariably accompanied by a shudder.

For although one has never witnessed a beheading and may not even be aware of the details, the imagination paints the horrifying picture and appropriately enough one's blood runs cold.

Death by decapitation was the method of execution granted to the nobility of many countries, for it was considered to be an honourable way in which to be dispatched. Common criminals were hanged, drowned, burned or otherwise disposed of, but royalty and the aristocracy were given the privilege of dying by an edged weapon, as in battle.

One of the first to be executed in this manner was Waltheof, Earl of Huntingdon, Northampton and Northumberland, in 1076, on the orders of William the Conqueror. He was beheaded by the sword, an execution weapon which in England was soon superseded by the axe.

But why beheading? Why not a sword thrust through the heart or lungs? Why not impaled on a lance? Well, when one stops to think about it, it is the head of a person which *is* that person. We recognize a friend by looking at his or her face. We talk to their faces, not their shoulders or feet. Photofit pictures of faces are used, not of hands or ankles. The head is the powerhouse, the control centre where all the thinking goes on, where emotional responses take place, and the rest of our body is simply the support system to keep our head and its processes nourished. Our hands are the conveying mechanism, and our legs are there to carry our heads, us, from place to place.

So because the head was the individual, it became obvious that the most effective way of removing an enemy of the State was to detach his or her head from his or her support system. That this belief was accepted in former times is evidenced by the fact that relatives of those executed sought to retrieve the severed heads of their loved ones, and not their bodies. Those heads were then kept by the family, just as if the executed one had returned home.

For instance, six days after the execution of Sir Thomas More, his daughter Margaret Roper claimed the head, which had been mummified by parboiling, from where it had been displayed on London Bridge, and kept it with her during her lifetime. At her death ten years later, it was placed with her coffin in the Roper tomb in St Dunstan's Church, Canterbury, 'in a niche in the wall, in a leaden box, something of the shape of a beehive, open in front, and with an iron grating before it', as the Reverend Bowes Bruce of Canterbury described it after inspecting the tomb in 1835.

In the 1970s the author and his wife, then living in the Tower of London only yards from the last resting place of Sir Thomas's body, visited St Dunstan's and after having partaken of the vicar's hospitality, were shown the entrance to the Roper tomb within the church. Shortly before our visit the tomb itself had been inspected by the authorities, who had been able to assure themselves that the saint's head in its casket still occupied its niche, alongside the coffins of the family.

Similarly in the case of Sir Walter Raleigh, executed at Old Palace Yard in Westminster on 29 October 1618. After the axe had done its work, it was reported by the historian Arthur Cayley that 'the head, after being shown on either side of the scaffold, was put into a leather bag, over which Sir Walter's gown was thrown, and the whole conveyed away in a mourning coach by Lady Raleigh'. It was preserved by her in a case during the twenty-nine years by which she survived her husband, and afterwards with no less piety by their affectionate son Carew, with whom it is supposed to have been buried at West Horsley, Surrey.

The weapon used in these and similar executions was known as the 'heading axe'. It was little more than an unwieldy chopper, and a close study of the one displayed in the Tower of London reveals the crudity of its manufacture, the lack of balance in its design. The blade, sixteen and a half inches long, broadens towards a convex cutting edge ten and a half inches wide. Apart from its sharpened edge, the blade is black and rough, just as it came from the blacksmith's forge. The weight of the heading axe, including the helve, is seven pounds fifteen ounces and its overall length about thirty-six inches.

It was of course an instrument of punishment, not mercy, so any refinements to improve its accuracy were considered completely unnecessary. The fact that it accomplished its task by crushing its brutal way through the vertebrae rather than by a clean cutting action was quite immaterial. If you didn't want to die that way, you'd better behave!

Its deadly partner on the scaffold was of course the block. Originally just any old chunk of oak, it soon evolved into a specific shape designed to help the executioner's task of decapitating the victim.

As it is essential that an object to be cut must rest firmly on something, it is obvious that the front of the neck, the throat, must be supported in order to strike a blow at the back of the neck. But a block of wood facilitating this would be so lacking in thickness that it would topple forward when the kneeling victim rested his or her throat on it. So the Home Office backroom boys of the day came up with a design which could hardly be improved on.

Rectangular in shape and wide enough to support the kneeling victim, it stood about two feet high, though some were lower, forcing the condemned person to lie down in an undignified position. Midway along each of the longer sides, at the upper edges, the wood was scooped out, wider at one side of the block than the other, so that the victim could push his or her shoulders in as far as possible. This positioned the throat, and therefore the neck, immediately above the flat area between the two hollows, with the chin resting in the narrower scoop and the head poised above the waiting basket of sawdust.

Incidentally, it is interesting to note that few if any types of execution involve the victim looking straight at the executioner. Death by the axe and guillotine require the victim to look down, death by the sword positions the victim at right angles to the executioner. Hanging and firing-squad methods call for blindfolds to be used and although this is explained as being merciful to the victim, psychologically one wonders how great an effort would be required to execute a person while looking into their eyes.

The block, then, its design perfected, went into operational use. Replacements were frequently needed, blocks splitting under the impact of repeated heavy blows. Such blows also reverberated through the planks of the scaffold, bouncing the victim off the block and spoiling the second axe stroke, should one be necessary. Accordingly, extra props were often positioned beneath the boards, but even this did not always solve the problem. As mentioned by General Williamson, Lieutenant of the Tower, when reporting on the execution of Lord Kilmarnock in 1746:

the block was at the desire of the Prisoner made two feet high, and I desired a good stiff upright post to be put just under it. It was then observed that Lord Kilmarnock's head being at one stroke seperated from the Body, all but a little flesh and skin, the body at the Stroke sprung backwards from the block and lay flatt on its back dead and extended, with its head fastned only by that little hold, which the Executioner chopt off or seperated on the scaffold. So that it is possible whenever the head is severed from the Body at one Stroke, it will allwais give that convulsive bounce or spring.

Sentences of death by the axe were not the only ones to involve severance of the head. If the crime had been high treason or similar, for which the sentence was to be hanged, drawn and quartered, an edged weapon was still a vital part of the proceedings, in more ways than one. For although the 'hanging' part of the sentence apparently deprived the victim of the privilege of decapitation, the details made it horrifyingly clear that beheading was indeed involved – and worse!

As pronounced by the Duke of Norfolk in 1521, on passing sentence on Edward, Duke of Buckingham, Lord High Constable of England:

> You shall be taken to the King's prison, the Tower of London, and there laid on a hurdle and so drawn to the place of execution, and there to be hanged and cut down alive; your members be cut off and cast into the fire; your bowels burnt before your eyes; your head smitten off and your body quartered and divided at the king's will. And God have mercy on your soul.

This ghastly method of execution, literally carving a man to pieces, was also symbolic in that he was, to put it delicately, simultaneously deprived of being able to father children who might follow in his traitorous footsteps.

One of the earliest victims of such barbaric punishment was Sir Andrew de Harcla, Earl of Carlisle, who was executed for treason. He and his 2,000 foot and mounted soldiers had stayed out of the battle when the Scots attacked and defeated the English at the Abbey of Byland and, his collusion with the enemy having been proved, a writ signed at Knaresborough, Yorkshire, on 27 February 1323, declared:

> that he should be stripped of his Earl's robes and ensigns of knighthood, his sword broken over his head, his gilt spurs hacked from his heels and that he should be drawn to the place of execution and there hanged by the neck; his heart, from whence came his treacherous thoughts,

together with his bowels, be taken out of his body, burnt to ashes and winnowed, his body cut into four quarters, one to be set up on the principal tower of Carlisle Castle, another on the tower of Newcastle upon Tyne, a third on the bridge of York, the fourth at Shrewsbury and his head on London Bridge.

Harcla's sister later petitioned Edward III for restitution of the remains for burial and His Majesty mercifully issued this order to de Lucy, the executioner:

The King, to his faithful and beloved Anthony de Lucy, Warden of Carlisle Castle, greetings. We command that you cause to be delivered without delay the quarter of the body of Andrew de Harcla, which hangs by the command of the Lord Edward, late King of England, our father, upon the walls of the said Castle, to our beloved Sarah, sister of the aforesaid Andrew, to whom we of our grace have granted that she may collect together the bones of the same Andrew and commit them to holy sepulchre whenever she wishes. And this you shall in no wise omit. Witness the King at York, 10 August 1337.

It is believed that the portions of the body so retrieved were subsequently buried in the ancient church of Kirkby Stephen, Cumbria, large marrowless bones being discovered interred there in 1847.

Another executioner's name appears later that century, being listed in the *Patent Rolls* of 8 July 1370:

Whereas it is certified in the Chancery by the Treasurer and Barons of the Exchequer that John de Warblyington, son and heir of Thomas de Warblyngton, made fine of Shirefield, County Southampton, which Thomas held in Chief on the date of his death by the service of being Marshall of the Prostitutes in the King's Household, dismembering condemned evil doers and measuring gallons and bushels in His Household.

More than a century elapses before another executioner is recorded, this one being named Cratwell or Gratwell. He was appointed in 1534 during the reign of Henry VIII, a busy time for one of his profession since it is known that under Henry's rule, over 72,000 people died on the scaffolds. Cratwell was notoriously cruel to his victims and even earned the praise of Sir Thomas Wriothesley, the Lord Chancellor, who described him as 'a conninge butcher in the quarteringe of men'.

As London's executioner at that time he could well have been the one who dispatched some of the famous of the day, such as Sir Thomas More and John Fisher, Bishop of Rochester. The lives of these two great men have filled many a book. Here we are considering their deaths.

On mounting the scaffold on Tower Hill, Sir Thomas forgave the executioner for what he had to do.

'Pluck up thy spirits, man, and be not afraid to do thine office,' he exclaimed. 'My neck is very short – take heed therefore thou strike not awry for saving thine honesty!'

He put his head on the block, telling the headsman to wait until he had put his beard aside, jocularly remarking that it had committed no treason. One blow of the axe was sufficient. His head was lovingly kept by his daughter Meg Roper, and buried with her, as earlier related.

John Fisher, Bishop of Rochester, was guilty of the same offence, that of failing to acknowledge that Henry VIII, rather than the Pope, was the supreme head of the Church of England. The bishop managed to communicate with the Vatican, and Paul III, against the express command of Henry VIII, promoted John Fisher and dispatched a cardinal's hat to him. On hearing of this, the King exclaimed with savage humour: ' 'Fore God then, he shall wear it on his shoulders!'

John Fisher was taken to Tower Hill, carried in a chair because of his weakened state. There, before a vast crowd, he was decapitated, his head afterwards being exhibited on London Bridge.

It might be wondered why London Bridge should be chosen as the prime site for such gory items. Well, for centuries, until Westminster Bridge was completed in 1750, London Bridge was the only link between London and the south, and so was known simply as The Bridge. It actually formed part of Watling Street, the Roman road which ran from the Channel coast through Kent, into

Southwark and the City, from where it continued north via St Albans. So all foot travellers, horsemen and coach passengers from the Continent and the populous south could enter London only by crossing its bridge. And on approaching the gatehouse which guarded its southern end, their attention would be drawn to the heads which, impaled on pikes, adorned its battlements. Paul Hentzner, a German traveller who frequently visited London during the reign of Elizabeth I, remarked that on one occasion he had counted no fewer than thirty heads grimacing on the gatehouse. A mute but effective warning to all those entering the City – watch your step or lose your head!

John Fisher, then, was executed on 22 June 1535, and it was reported that instead of the head being placed on the bridge the same day, it was first taken to be shown to Anne Boleyn. Her reactions at the sight of her opponent's severed head are not recorded.

The next day, however, as Dr Thomas Baily wrote in 1665:

> The head, being parboiled, was pricked upon a pole and set high on London Bridge. And here I cannot omit to declare unto you the miraculous sight of this head which, after it had stood up the space of fourteen days upon the bridge, could not be perceived to waste nor consume; neither for the weather, which was then very hot, neither for the parboiling, but it grew daily fresher and fresher, so that in his lifetime he never looked so well, for his cheeks being beautified with a comely red, the face looked as that it had beholden the people passing by, and would have spoken to them; which many took to be a miracle that Almighty God showed the innocence and holiness of this blessed father. Wherefore the people coming daily to see this strange sight, the passage over the bridge was so stopped with their coming and going that almost no cart nor horse could pass. Therefore at the end of fourteen daies the executioner was ordered to take down the head at night and throw it into the River of Thames.

The reference to 'parboiling' requires some explanation. This was a process applied to severed heads in order to preserve them for as long as possible from the ravages of the weather and the attention of hungry sea birds. The recipe used by the executioner required him to parboil the heads in a large kettle or cauldron which also contained salt and cumin seed, the latter condiment rendering the flesh unappetizing to the gulls.

But to return to executioner Cratwell. He lasted only four years in office, meeting his Maker on 1 September 1538, the Sunday following St Bartholomew's Day. As Hall reported in his *Chronicles*, Cratwell 'was hanged at the wrestling place on the backsyde of Clerkenwel besyde London, for robbing of a bouthe in Bartholomew's Fayre, at which execution was above 20,000 people attending'. Cratwell, of all people, should have known better.

Another fellow-craftsman who met the same fate was known as Stumpleg. He it was who, wearing a white apron, beheaded the Duke of Northumberland on 22 August 1553. The victim wore a white damask gown, elegant apparel befitting his rank and dignity.

The proud Duke had been adviser to young King Edward VI, a position of great influence. With an eye to the future, he arranged for one of his sons, Guildford Dudley, to marry the King's cousin Lady Jane Grey. Edward, a sickly child, decreed that Jane should succeed to the throne rather than his royal half-sister Mary, and not long after that the young king died of consumption.

Northumberland, his dream of prestige and power now within his reach, promptly proclaimed his daughter-in-law Jane, Queen of England. But the country supported Mary's claim so overwhelmingly that the Duke was a doomed man, and so met his death on the scaffold.

Guildford Dudley died in the same way on Tower Hill, his remains being brought back for burial in the Chapel Royal of St Peter ad Vincula within the Tower. As the hurdle, bearing its gruesome burden, was carried across Tower Green, Lady Jane Grey, now a widow, was led out to the private scaffold by the Chapel. Reportedly she burst into tears at the sight but quickly regained her composure as she mounted the straw-covered scaffold.

There her gentlewomen removed her gown, neckerchief and *frose paste* (a matronly headdress, the words later evolving into 'frow's piece' and eventually to 'frontispiece', as in a book). Prayers were said and then Jane knelt before the block. Apprehensively she said, 'Will you take my head off before I lay me down?' The executioner, described as a very tall man dressed in a tight-fitting suit of black wool, and made even more terrifying by the hood and hideous mask he wore, reassured her.

She tied the kerchief over her eyes. Then reaching out she exclaimed, 'What shall I do? Where is it, where is it?' A weeping companion guided her and, as she bent her neck, the axe descended on the young queen of nine days. Her corpse was buried next to that of her husband in the Chapel Royal, between the coffins of the other two queens, Anne Boleyn and Catherine Howard, who had also perished on Tower Green. The heads of all three were not held high for the spectators' morbid gaze, but were placed with their bodies in the coffins.

Jane's executioner was disguised in hood and mask not to add terror to the scene but in order to prevent recognition, a practice followed by many of his trade. Some carried it further, strapping large oval baskets to their backs, these medieval flak jackets having the added advantage of warding off brickbats thrown by their victims' sympathizers. Such disguises were necessary, for an executioner doing his duty could later be classed as a traitor, to be hunted down by the authorities when the opposition gained the ascendancy. Even executing common criminals could be dangerous, the hangman himself becoming extremely unpopular with the deceased's vengeful friends. Anonymous executioners lived longer!

Eleven days after Jane's death, her father, Henry Grey, Duke of Suffolk, also mounted the scaffold steps, before large crowds on Tower Hill. As the grim drama unfolded, the axe did its work, the executioner then holding the head up high and proclaiming loudly, 'Behold the head of a traitor! So die all traitors!'

This brandishing of the severed head, as well as being somewhat of a vindictive gesture, was essential in those pre-photography days, in order to assure everybody that the person sentenced to death had actually been executed. Were it done surreptitiously, an impostor might well emerge later and, by professing to be the 'victim', claim all his titles and estates.

The Duke's head was retrieved, either from the coffin or from London Bridge, probably by his widow, and because the family had a mansion close to the Tower, in what is now a street called the Minories, it was buried in a vault near the altar of their private chapel.

As the centuries passed, much rebuilding took place in the area, the Greys' chapel and house eventually being demolished and replaced by the Church of the Holy Trinity. And in 1851 the head was discovered in a small vault on the south side of the church altar. It was thickly encrusted with oak sawdust from the scaffold basket into which it had fallen, the tannin in the oak having preserved the head.

It was examined by Sir George Scharf, Keeper of the National Portrait Gallery, who stated that its features corresponded to those in contemporary portraits, and a medical authority, Doctor Mouat, assessed it:

> as belonging to a man past the prime of life, and that the head was removed by rapid decapitation during life admits of no doubt. A large gaping gash, which had not divided the subcutaneous structures, shows that the first stroke of the axe was misdirected, too near the occiput, and in a slanting direction. The retraction of the skin, the violent convulsive action of the muscles, and the formation of a cup-like cavity with the body of the spinal bone at the base, prove that the severance was effected during life, and in cold weather.

The church was closed down in 1899 and the relic of Henry Grey, Queen Jane's father, was transferred to St Botolph's Church, Aldgate. There, earlier this century, it was possible, by courtesy of the vicar, to view the head in its airtight glass container. It was described by Sir George Younghusband in his book *The Tower of London*:

There is no shrinkage of the face, the eyes are wide open, and the eyeballs and pupils perfectly preserved, though of a parchment colour. The skin, too, all over is of the same yellowish hue. When first found, the hair of the head and beard were still on, but owing to its very brittle state and from being handled by several people, these broke off, though in a strong light the bristles may still be seen. The nose is not quite perfect, but the ears are practically as in life. The head had evidently been severed by two heavy blows, and loose skin, jagged and looking like loose parchment, demonstrates where the severance occurred.

When, with ghoulish curiosity, the author of this book visited the church in the 1970s, the verger explained that the macabre relic had been reverently interred beneath the paving stones at the church's entrance. Henry Grey's head had finally been laid to rest in consecrated ground, a mere arrow's flight from his daughter's grave in the Tower of London.

Two years after the Duke's death, in 1556, executioner Stumpleg fell foul of the law himself. Caught thieving, he was condemned to death and hanged at Tyburn where, as the diarist Machyn pointed out, 'he himself had hangyd many a man, and quartered many, and had beheded many a nobulman'.

A distinction should be made here between Tower Hill and Tyburn. Most of those who suffered on the former were aristocrats; Tower Hill could be described as the Wimbledon of executions, where only the seeded players of society appeared. Tyburn, on the other hand, was very much the Wembley of the day. In football parlance, any team of players, no matter how humble, could perform there, be they highwaymen, robbers, murderers or just petty thieves. There stood the gallows for hanging, the scaffold for beheading and dismembering, performances being presented regularly, from the year 1196 until transferred to Newgate Prison in 1783.

The site of Tyburn was of great significance. Just as one wouldn't erect an advertising hoarding in a quiet cul-de-sac, so one wouldn't deter many potential wrongdoers by locating a scaffold down a lonely lane. And so, in the same way as those entering London from the south took due notice of the heads displayed on London Bridge, so others approaching the City from the north-west, along the same major road, were equally reminded of their civic responsibilities by the sight of Tyburn's scaffold and gallows, and its corpse-laden gibbets.

In its earlier days the execution site was known as 'The Elms', as were other sites at Smithfield, Covent Garden and elsewhere, this particular type of tree being considered the tree of justice by the Normans. Indeed, the stream called the Ty-bourn, flowing through a wide area of rough ground, was originally bordered by a row of elms.

The exact position of the scaffold is impossible to determine, as from 1759 it ceased to be a fixture but was assembled as required. It would certainly seem however, to have been positioned at the junction of Edgware Road (Watling Street) and Oxford Street/Bayswater Road, adjacent to Marble Arch. At the junction of Edgeware Road and Oxford Street is a small traffic island, where the more daring readers will find set in its stones a symbolic plaque bearing the words: 'Here stood Tyburn Tree, Removed 1759'. Should the unwary investigator not heed the dense traffic thereabouts, yet another tombstone would be inscribed 'Died at Tyburn'!

Those destined for a Tyburn execution were brought from the Tower of London or Newgate Prison (where now stands the Old Bailey Central Criminal Court), their journey on a hurdle or by cart enriching the English language with such phrases as 'gone west' and 'in the cart'.

Until 1571 the gallows were quite basic, consisting of two uprights and a cross-piece, but on 1 June of that year a much improved design was introduced. This was the Triple Tree which, having three uprights and cross-beams, could accommodate up to twenty-four occupants simultaneously.

Its first victim was Dr John Story, a Roman Catholic noted for his persecution of Protestants during the reign of Queen Mary. Upon her death he, fearful of retribution, enlisted the aid of the Spanish ambassador's chaplain and fled to Flanders, where he obtained a lucrative post with the Customs at Antwerp.

But Protestant memories were long. One day in August 1570 Parker, owner of an English ship, lured Story on board to inspect the cargo. Once the doctor was below decks, the hatches were battened down, the anchor raised, and the ship set sail for Yarmouth.

The captive was taken to the Tower and duly tried and sentenced to death. Because he had lived in Spain at one time, the Spanish ambassador tried to save him by claiming that he was a Spanish subject, to which Queen Elizabeth is said to have retorted: 'The King of Spain may have his head if he wants it, but his body shall be left in England!'

And so, as stated in the *Harleian Manuscripts*, 'the first day of June 1571 the said John Story was drawn upon a herdell from the Tower unto Tyborn, wher was prepared for him a new payre of gallows made in triangular manner'. He was cut down while still alive and it is reported that while the executioner was 'rifling through his bowels' Story sat up and dealt him a blow, before being quickly dismembered.

The sixteenth century saw heads falling like swathes of poppies under the scythe, one in particular being that of an elderly lady, Margaret Pole, Countess of Salisbury, who suffered the full fury of Henry VIII's wrath. This proud Plantagenet had four sons, one of whom, Cardinal Pole, denounced Henry's supremacy and divorce from Catherine of Aragon. Henry, determined to wipe out the entire family, imprisoned the Countess and other relatives in the Tower and there she was held, without trial, warmth or adequate clothing, for two years, until on 27 May 1541 she was led out to Tower Green.

A ghastly scene followed for, in the words of Lord Herbert:

> she was commanded to lay her head on the block but she (as a person of great quality assured me) refused, saying 'So should traitors do, and I am none.'

Neither did it serve that the executioner told her it was the fashion [necessary]; so turning her grey head every way, shee bid him if hee would have her hedd, to get it off as best he could; so that he was constrained to fetch it off slovenly.

Many strokes were necessary to the Countess's head and shoulders before the merciful end came, her remains then being buried before the altar in the Chapel Royal.

While imprisoned, the Countess had been sent clothing by Queen Catherine Howard: 'a nightdress furred, a kirtle of worsted, a petticoat, furred. A nightgown lined with satin of eyprus, and faced with satin. A bonnet, four pairs of hose, four pairs of shoes and some slippers', as listed in the Queen's household expenses. Little did Catherine realize that in less than a year's time, she too would lose her head on Tower Green.

Accused by enemies at Court of 'dalliance with others', she was charged with treason. Frantically she sought to speak with her husband, but was seized by the guards. Despite her piercing screams, heard all over Hampton Court Palace, Henry refused to see her. Today the Haunted Gallery there is so called because of the supernatural presence of the doomed queen.

Awaiting death in the Tower, nevertheless the young, 22-year-old girl recovered her composure. Like so many others before her who had shown dignity and calmness on the scaffold, she was determined that she would not give way beneath the strain. Incredibly then, on the eve of her execution, she asked that the block be brought to her room and the executioner summoned to attend.

Whilst the officers of the Tower watched the macabre rehearsal, Queen Catherine knelt and laid her head in the hollow of the block, to assure herself that she could now go through the ordeal with fortitude. And at 10 a.m. on the next day, 15 February 1542, her head, and that of her lady-in-waiting Lady Rochford, fell beneath the axe.

But Catherine was not the last queen to be beheaded in England. In 1586 Mary, Queen of Scots, Queen Dowager of France, posed a threat to the English Throne, a challenge so persistent that Elizabeth I took drastic action. Mary was placed on trial, found guilty and condemned to death. As a rare departure from the usual practice, the place of execution was to be indoors, the venue being Fotheringhay Castle, Northamptonshire (now regrettably a ruin) in the great hall of which had been erected the scaffold, two feet high, twelve feet long, with rails around its edges and draped with black cloth.

In the presence of officers of the Court and ministers of the Church, Mary's ladies-in-waiting prepared her for the ordeal. The removal of her black robes revealed a red velvet petticoat and silk scarlet bodice. Discarding her petticoat, she donned a pair of scarlet satin sleeves over her kirtle, exclaiming that 'she had never such grooms to make her unready, and that she had never put off her clothes in such a company!'

Kneeling down on the cushion, she prayed, and positioned her neck on the block. A hush fell on the spectators as Bull, the executioner, stepped forward. As recorded in *State Papers Domestic* he had arranged for his assistant, 'the bloody and unseemly varlet attending upon him', to hold down Mary's arms. Even so, whether unnerved by the imposing assembly or just inaccurate, Bull's aim went awry. His first blow struck the back of the Queen's head, providentially stunning her. Again the axe fell, this time virtually severing her head.

Ever mindful of the need to prove that justice had indeed been done, the Queen's head was then washed and placed on a velvet cushion at one of the windows overlooking the courtyard, in full view of the crowds gathered there. After a short while it was taken, together with the body, to an upper chamber, there to be embalmed by surgeons. This process was very necessary, in view of the fact that nearly six months would elapse before her burial on 1 August 1587. She was interred at Peterborough, the grave-digger being Old Scarlett, a sturdy, bearded fellow who, it is reported, also buried Queen Catherine of Aragon. A quarter of a century later, the Scottish Queen's remains were re-interred in the more historic surrounds of Westminster Abbey.

During those years many others, Jesuits in particular, were persecuted and oppressed. One priest was Robert Sutton who, as an Anglican rector at Lutterworth in Leicestershire in 1571, was converted to Catholicism by his brother William. Caught, he was hanged at Clerkenwell, London, in 1588, afterwards being drawn and quartered, probably by executioner Bull.

Sutton's remains were duly exhibited as a deterrent, and some were retrieved as holy relics. John Gerard, a Jesuit priest famous for his daring flight from imprisonment in the Tower, possessed one of these:

> a forefinger of the martyr which, by wonderful providence of God, together with the thumb, was preserved from decay, although the whole arm had been pinned up to be eaten by the birds. When some Catholics came to remove it secretly (it had been exposed for a whole year) they found nothing but bones. The only parts still covered with flesh and skin were the thumb and forefinger which had been anointed at ordination and had been sanctified by the touch of the Blessed Sacrament. His brother William, another good priest, kept the thumb in his possession and presented me with the forefinger.

Holy relics were also obtained after the execution of Jesuit Edmund Campion who, found guilty of plotting against Queen Elizabeth, was hanged, drawn and quartered at Tyburn on 20 December 1581. Despite every effort to prevent sympathizers from gaining possession of limbs and items of clothing, one of Father Campion's arms was later retrieved from where it had been displayed on the city gates and preserved reverently by fellow Catholics. Another priest, Father Parsons, managed to procure the noose with which Edmund Campion had been half hanged, and wore it about his own neck in holy memory.

A precious relic now revered by the nuns of Tyburn Convent is the forearm of Blessed Thomas Maxfield, a missionary priest executed on the nearby gallows on 1 July 1616. So sympathetic was the crowd towards him that garlands of flowers festooned the grim structure and he was allowed to meet his death on the rope rather than by the subsequent knife.

Many heads and quarters did in fact remain *in situ* for a number of years, until they disintegrated into dust, fell or were blown down. Some, however, turned up in the most unexpected places. After the Great Fire of 1666, which devastated London, whole areas of houses and streets had to be cleared of debris. Stowe's *Survey of London* reported the bizarre discovery made by workmen clearing rubble from an old cellar in Blackfriars:

> They came to an old wall of great thickness, where appeared a kind of cupboard. Which being opened, there was found in it four Pots or Cases of fine Pewter, thick, with Covers of the same, and Rings fastened on the top to take up [lift] or put down at pleasure. The Cases were flat before and rounded behind. And in each of them were reposited a human head, unconsumed by the fire, preserved as it seems by Art; with their teeth and Hair, the Flesh of a tawny Colour, wrap't up in black silk, almost consumed. And a certain Substance, of a blackish colour, crumbled into dust, lying at the bottom of the Pots.
>
> One of these Pots, with the Head in it, I saw in October 1703, being in the custody of Mr Prestbury, then Sope Maker in Smithfield. The Pot was inscribed on the inside of the cover in a scrawling Character (which might be used in the times of Henry VIII) 'J. CORNELIUS'. This Head was without any neck, having short red Hair upon it, thick, and it could not be pulled off; and yellow hair upon the temples; a little bald on top, perhaps a Tonsure, the forepart of the Nose sunk, the Mouth gaping, ten sound teeth, others had been plucked out; the skin like tanned leather, the Features of the Face visible. There was one body found near it, buried, and without a Head. But no other Bodies found. The three other Heads had some of the Necks joined to them and had broader and plainer Razure; which showed to be Priests. These three Heads are now dispersed. One was given to an Apothecary, another entrusted with the Parish Clerk who, it is thought, got money by shewing of it. It is probable that they were at last privately procured and conveyed abroad, and now become Holy Relics.

Who these were, there is no record as I know of, nor had

any of them Names inscribed but one. To me they seem to have been some zealous Priests or Friers, executed for treason; whereof there were many in the Rebellion in Lincolnshire about 1538, or for denying the King's Supremacy. And their remains were here privately deposited by the Black Friers.

Subsequent research by historian Dr Challoner and others revealed the identity of John Cornelius. He was a Jesuit priest, born in 1557 who, after studying at Oxford and later joining the church in Rome, became a Roman Catholic chaplain in England in 1583. There he travelled the country, bringing spiritual guidance and comfort to the persecuted Catholics during Elizabeth's reign.

Constantly pursued by the authorities he, like his brother priests, had to be prepared to conceal himself at a moment's notice in the priest-holes, secret hiding places ingeniously constructed in the country houses, behind panelling, under stairways and even fireplaces, for days on end, without food or water. Cramped in little more than small cupboards, not daring to move or make a sound, their endurance can only be admired.

The searchers, known as pursuivants, were cunning and expert. Counting windows inside and out would reveal a hidden room; measuring adjoining rooms could disclose secret cavities. Panelling was tapped, the sounds identifying hollow spaces behind, and should all these measures fail, the searchers would loudly discuss their disappointment and intended departure. Then creeping back, they would impersonate the house servants, tapping on the walls and joyfully announcing to the fugitives that the coast was clear, that they could now come out to stretch their limbs, to eat and drink.

And so it was that John Cornelius, visiting the widow of Sir John Arundel, in April 1594, in order to perform Mass, was betrayed by a disloyal (or law-abiding?) servant of the house and had hastily to seek refuge when the pursuivants arrived. While some of the searchers made much commotion in one part of the house, others waited elsewhere, quietly listening. And on hearing Cornelius cough, they broke down the panelling and arrested him.

As he was being led away a relative of the family, Mr Bosgrave, seeing the priest was hatless, put his own hat on the priest's head. He too was promptly arrested, as were two servants, Terence Carey and Patrick Salmon, for not reporting the presence of the priest.

Cornelius was taken to London and there racked to make him divulge the whereabouts of other Jesuits and on his refusal he was tried and found guilty. On 4 July 1594 Bosgrave, Carey and Salmon were hanged and Father Cornelius hanged, drawn and quartered, his head afterwards being nailed to the gallows. It was later retrieved by fellow Catholics and given to London's Black Friars as a holy relic. There, stored with others in the crypt, it was revered until, more than sixty years later, the Great Fire reduced the buildings to rubble, leaving the caskets with their gruesome contents unscathed underground.

Soon after the beginning of the seventeenth century, new aristocrats of the axe graced the scaffold. The Brandons, father and son, assumed command from 1611 until 1649, a momentous period in England's history. The elder, Gregory Brandon, claimed to be of noble descent and in fact the historian and author Richard Davey stated in his book *The Tower of London* that he had in his possession an ancient document dated 1692 showing armorial bearings which attested to the fact that Gregory's father was the illegitimate son of Charles Brandon, Duke of Suffolk. The Duke, brother-in-law to Henry VIII, fathered Henry Grey whose child was Lady Jane Grey. Gregory the hangman could therefore claim some vaguely royal connection, albeit on the wrong side of the blanket!

Whether this story was common knowledge at the time, or whether the members of the College of Heralds indulged in practical jokes on each other is not known, but *State Papers Domestic*, series 1611–18, states: 'January 1617 Ralph Brooke, York Herald, played a trick on Sir William Segar, Garter King of Arms, by sending him a coat of arms drawn up for Gregory Brandon, said to be a merchant of London and well descended, which Garter subscribed [authorized] and then found out that Brandon was the hangman; Garter and York are both imprisoned, one for foolery, the other for knavery.'

Such a coat of arms entitled the holder to the title of 'Esquire', a considerable honour in those days and one which could be handed down to one's successors. Not that this earned him much respect, though, for Brandon Esquire was more familiarly known as 'Old Gregory' to the public at large.

He started his hanging apprenticeship by assisting executioner Derrick, and may even have been present at the butchery inflicted on Guy Fawkes and his colleagues in 1606, for such multiple executions were too much for one man, two or more assistants being required.

As the official executioner Gregory Brandon not only dispatched such missionary priests as William Scot, Richard Newport and Thomas Maxfield, all hanged, drawn and quartered, but achieved notoriety for executing Sir Walter Raleigh in Old Palace Yard, Westminster. The burning of heretics at Smithfield, London, also fell to his lot, as did the routine whipping and branding.

He died in 1640, his office as chief executioner going to his son Richard, a young man better known to the aficionados of the gallows as 'Young Gregory', and with a family upbringing such as his, it was inevitable that he would adopt his father's profession. Never was the phrase 'a chip off the old block' more applicable!

Richard obviously intended to be proficient in his new career, for it is reported that while still a youngster he practised by decapitating dogs and cats. True or not, Richard always prided himself on his skill with the axe and boasted that he never needed to strike more than once, a claim that would seem to have been confirmed by available records.

He was just as skilful with the knife and cleaver, for Jesuit priests were still being hunted and executed. On 1 February 1645 Father Henry Morse was hanged, drawn and quartered at Tyburn, the Portuguese ambassador Don Antonio de Sousa and his French counterpart the Marquis de Sabran witnessing the barbaric ceremony. 'His bosom was laid open,' wrote the Marquis later, 'his heart torn out, his entrails burned and his body quartered.' Then their footmen came forward to dip their masters' handkerchiefs in the martyr's blood as holy souvenirs.

The French and Spanish ambassadors also interceded on behalf of another priest, Father John Southworth, but to no avail, and he was executed at Tyburn on 28 June 1654, his mummified remains being kept and revered in St George's Chapel, Westminster Cathedral, London.

In the early 1640s however, the power struggle between King Charles I and Parliament had started and the Commons, backed by public opinion, was gaining the upper hand. Close advisers and aristocratic friends of the King were accused of treason and, being found guilty, were delivered into Brandon's hands. In those years many heads fell into the basket on the scaffold, among them those of the Earl of Holland, Lord Strafford, the Marquis of Hamilton, even William Laud, Archbishop of Canterbury.

Such was the anti-royal mood of the public that each scaffold appearance by Brandon was wildly applauded by the crowd. Indeed, following the execution of Lord Strafford, the spectators from out of town rode home triumphantly, waving their hats and shouting 'His head is off, his head is off!' and any householder failing to celebrate around the bonfires had his windows broken. Just like today's soccer hooligans!

But all these aristocratic executions were but rehearsals for the one which surely was the climax of Richard Brandon's career, the beheading of Charles I. Queens of England and Scotland had perished beneath the axe, but until 30 January 1649, monarchs had been the ones who sent *others* to the scaffold.

The King's trial is now history. The findings and sentence were confirmed by the Commons, who further ordered that the execution axe be brought from the Tower of London in readiness.

The warrant was brutally plain and unambiguous:

Whereas Charles Stuart, King of England, is and standeth convicted, attainted and condemned of High Treason and other High Crimes; and sentence upon Saturday last was pronounced against him by this Court, to be put to death by the severing of his head from his body; of which Sentence execution yet remaineth to be done.

These are therefore to will and require you to see the said Sentence executed, in the open Street before Whitehall, upon the morrow, being the thirtieth day of this instant month January between the hours of Ten in the morning and Five in the afternoon, with full effect. And for so doing, this shall be your Warrant.

And these are to require all Officers and Soldiers and other Good People of the Nation of England, to be assisting unto you on this Service. Given under our Hands and Seals, John Bradshaw, Thomas Grey, Oliver Cromwell (and fiftysix others).

The next morning Charles walked from St James's Palace to the Banqueting House in Whitehall, escorted by a Regiment of Foot with drums beating and flags flying, and also his private guard of partisans, the Yeomen of the Guard. He was dressed in a suit of black satin, with a short velvet coat, his sombre dress contrasting not only with the gold cane he carried, but with the brilliance of his personal jewellery, for in addition to his ear-rings he wore a large pearl surmounted by a gold crown, together with the decoration of the Order of the George and Garter.

Meanwhile Richard Brandon, having shown some hesitancy at the task to be done, was 'fetched out of bed by a troop of horse' and escorted to the scaffold.

At 2 p.m. the King was conducted through one of the large windows of the Banqueting House on to a large, black, draped platform which projected out into Whitehall, a dais visible to the thousands who filled the streets and surrounding windows, some even clinging to roof tops and chimneys.

Two masked men dressed entirely in black now awaited the King, one seemingly old, with a grey beard, the other a young, fair-haired man. Such was the aversion felt by so many at the actual beheading of a king, whatever his dissolute or arrogant ways, that the executioners had prudently taken precautions, disguising themselves to avoid future repercussions. Their masks and false beards, together with thick coats, disguised them so effectively that at the Restoration of the Monarchy eleven years later, vengeful royalists accused a captain in the Commonwealth Army, William Hewlet, of being responsible. On 13 June 1660 Hewlet was committed to the Tower and on 15 October that year condemned to death, but no record of his fate has survived.

There is no doubt, however, that it was Richard Brandon who waited with the axe that day, his assistant being William Lowen, a former dunghill-cleaner. The King, on seeing that the block was only ten inches high, objected, for it would require him to lie humiliatingly prone instead of in a kneeling position. Brandon replied, 'It can be no higher, Sir', omitting to explain that the low block, and the four staples driven into the surrounding boards, were there to facilitate binding the King down, should he refuse to submit.

Charles gave his gold cane and George decoration to Bishop Juxon and said 'Remember!', the significance of which has never been understood. Of the numerous watches he carried, he gave a silver one to the Duke of Richmond and a gold one for the Duchess. Sir Thomas Herbert received the silver alarm watch usually kept next to the royal bed, and a fourth one Charles gave to his close companion John Ashburnham.

The King then told Brandon not to strike until he gave the signal by stretching out his arms, to which the executioner answered, 'I will, an't please Your Majesty.'

The white satin cap was next donned, the King saying to Brandon, 'Does my hair trouble you?' As it was essential that the royal neck was clearly visible when the time came, the Bishop assisted the executioner to tuck all the flowing locks under the cap. Finally the King urged Brandon to do his work cleanly and not put him to pain, to which the executioner, obviously overcome by the enormity of the task, could only nod.

Charles lay down full length and, positioning his neck, started to pray. Then, aware that Brandon stood over him with the axe poised high, called out 'Wait for the sign! Wait for the sign!' There was a pause. Then suddenly the

King spread his arms wide, the rapid movement coinciding with Brandon's instantaneous reaction as the executioner brought the heavy weapon down with deadly accuracy. 'Thus sodanly with one bloe his head sped from his shoulders', a shocked witness recorded; 'and a universal groan, the like never before heard, broke from the dense and countless multitude', wrote John Timbs in his book *Romance of London*.

The horror was further increased when the assistant hangman William Lowen picked up the severed head and, displaying it to the massed onlookers, shouted 'Behold the head of a traitor!'

The head and body were placed in a coffin and, after having been embalmed by Mr Trapham, a surgeon, the corpse was taken to the Palace of Whitehall. There, in the King's sleeping chamber, the public were admitted, to file past and pay their respects. A slanderous story was circulated at the time that Cromwell also came, cold-bloodedly lifting the head to make sure that it was really severed from the body!

On 7 February the King's remains were taken to St George's Chapel, Windsor, the officials paying the sum of five shillings and sixpence to Isaac the sexton and Widow Puddifat for unlocking the chapel doors. The vault was located by those present stamping on the stone floor, hollow sounds determining where the flagstones should be lifted.

Within the vault the mourners found two coffins, one large lead one containing, as they had surmised, the remains of Henry VIII, shreds of a purple pall still adhering to its lid. The other, a smaller one, was that of Jane Seymour, his third wife, who died soon after the birth of their son Edward VI.

Denied a burial service, the coffin of Charles I was placed next to them, a strip of soft lead inscribed 'King Charles 1648' being attached to its lid, and a black velvet pall draped over the coffin, before the vault was once more sealed up.

A hundred and sixty-five years later, in 1813, the coffin was accidentally exposed when part of the vault was opened. On lifting the lid Charles's body was seen to be covered with a cerecloth, and the severed head had been carefully adjusted to the shoulders. The King's face was as perfect as when he had been alive, the oval shape of the head, the pointed beard, being identical to those in the Vandyke portraits.

The fissure made by the axe was clearly visible, the flesh at its edge blackened and torn. The back of the head and the place where it rested in the coffin was stained with what was obviously blood.

Sir Henry Halford, who accompanied the Prince Regent viewing the remains, cut off a lock of the King's hair and later presented part of it, set in a golden locket, to the novelist Sir Walter Scott. It was also reported that he retained the late King's fourth cervical vertebra, which he used as a salt cellar on his dining table for nearly thirty years until word of its existence reached Queen Victoria. Her Majesty, finding it far from amusing, ordered it to be returned and so, in a small casket, it was replaced in the tomb within St George's Chapel.

After the execution Richard Brandon got his remuneration: '£30 for his pains, all in half crowns, within an hour of striking the blow, plus an orange stuck full of cloves and a handkerchief from the King's pocket'. He sold the orange for ten shillings to a neighbour on Rosemary Lane, and one wonders whether he gave the royal handkerchief to his wife Mary as a souvenir.

Later that year, the executioner began to complain of feeling ill and his health started to deteriorate. He took to his bed and, on Sunday 20 June 1649, he died at his home on Tower Hill. The actual cause is not recorded though some say that 'he died of remorse at killing a king'.

He was buried in the churchyard of St Mary Matfelon, in Alder Street, Whitechapel, and an entry in the burial register describes him as 'Richard Brandon, a man out of Rosemary Lane. This R. Brandon is supposed to have cut off the head of Charles the First'. True to his boast, one blow of the axe was sufficient and for that alone his victims should have been grateful.

The restoration of Charles II to the throne heralded a

wave of revenge against all those responsible for his father's execution, in particular those who had dared to sit in judgement on him. It was time for not only the pendulum to swing, but also the axe! Of those branded as regicides, some had died, others had fled to the Continent. But retribution knew no barriers; all would pay the price.

The London executioner at that time was Edward Dun, who lived in the City's Cripplegate district. He chose to be known as 'Squire' Dun, claiming that he was entitled to, because he executed those who had betrayed their country. His reputation for cruelty was well earned, for he was even known to taunt his victims on the scaffold and, never averse to an extra income would, for a fee, allow those sentenced to be hanged, drawn and quartered, to die on the rope before being cut down.

In all probability he it was who performed the more gruesome operations decreed by the courts, gruesome because three of the King's judges had died earlier – Oliver Cromwell, his son-in-law Henry Ireton, and John Bradshaw, Lord President of the trial court. All three had been buried in magnificent tombs in the Henry VII Chapel of Westminster Abbey, but their eternal rest was rudely disturbed. Their corpses were exhumed and, to quote Sir George Wharton in an account written in 1662:

> The odious carcasses of O. Cromwell, H. Ireton and J. Bradshaw were drawn upon sledges to Tyburn on the anniversary of the execution of Charles I and, being pulled out of their Coffins, there hanged at the several angles of that Triple Tree till Sunset. Then taken down, beheaded, and their loathsome Truncks thrown into a deep hole beneath the gallows. Their heads were afterwards set upon Poles on the top of Westminster Hall.

An interesting footnote to the above was reported in *The Times* of 9 May 1860, concerning excavations at the Tyburn site on Edgware Road. Workmen uncovered a quantity of bones, obviously the remains of those who had swung on Tyburn Tree. Since the bodies and limbs of most victims were taken away for dissection or display, it is possible that those unearthed could have been the remains of the three Roundheads whose bodies had been so maltreated.

The heads of the three regicides remained on top of Westminster Hall, staring through sightless eyes over the City, until they were dislodged during the Great Storm of 1703. Cromwell's head, it was reported, was found by a sentry sheltering from the storm and he kept it until a friend sold it to a family called Russell.

Sir Joshua Reynolds tried to acquire it, but in 1787 it was bought by James Fox, an antiquarian dealer who put it on public display, his advertisement in the *Morning Chronicle* of 18 March 1799 proclaiming;

> The Real Embalmed Head of the Powerful and Renowned Usurper Oliver Cromwell, is now exhibited at 5 Mead Court, Old Bond Street, where the rattlesnake was shown last year; a genuine narrative relating to its Acquisition, concealment and Preservation is to be had at the Place of Exhibition. Tickets Half a Crown.

By 1865 the head had passed into the possession of Mr W A Wilkinson of Beckenham, Kent. John Timbs FSA described how the iron spike that passed through it,

> is worn, in the part above the crown of the head almost as thin as a bodkin by having been subjected to the variations of the weather, but the part within the skull which is protected by its situation, is not much corroded. The woodwork [the shaft of the pike] part of which remains, is so much worm-eaten that it cannot be touched without crumbling. The countenance has been compared by Mr Flaxman, the statuary, with a plaster cast of Oliver's face taken after his death, of which there are several in London, and he declares the features are perfectly similar.

In 1932 the head, still in the possession of the Wilkinsons, was sent to the London University, where Professor Karl Pearson and others were producing a book illustrating every known picture of Cromwell.

The expert opinion of the renowned Master of the Tower Armouries, Charles Ffoulkes, was sought as to the authenticity of the spike involved. He determined that because of its design it was indeed a seventeenth-century fighting weapon, and after a further examination had revealed that a worm-hole had penetrated both the broken shaft and the skull, he had little doubt that head and pike had been aligned in that position for over two centuries.

Following a far-ranging analysis of records, measurements, pictures and sculptures of the subject, the professor and his staff concluded that the head was almost certainly that of the late Lord Protector, Oliver Cromwell.

The three dead regicides, hanged and mutilated, nevertheless endured none of the agonies suffered by their living colleagues when reaping the wrath of the Royalists. One was Major General Thomas Harrison, found guilty and sentenced to death. The gallows had been erected in front of Trafalgar Square, where King Charles's statue now stands, and Harrison mounted the scaffold, the noose about his neck. Within minutes the rope was tightened, only to be released so that the half-strangled victim could be eviscerated. The executioner, presumably Squire Dun, sliced open Harrison's abdomen and, tearing out the bowels, hurled them on to the fire. Then, to the amazement of the crowd, Harrison is said to have leant forward and struck his tormentor over the head!

The awful sentence was completed, although despite the quarters being exhibited on the city gates, the head was retained for a particularly macabre purpose. Ironically the Roundhead General's republican principles lived on, for one of his sons escaped to America where he settled and raised a family. And in 1891, little more than two centuries after Thomas Harrison's execution, his direct descendant General Benjamin Harrison was elected the twenty-third President of the United States of America.

Another to suffer on the Royalist scaffold was John Cook, Solicitor General of the Commonwealth, who conducted the trial against Charles I. Tied to a hurdle, he had the added horror of having his friend Harrison's gory head fixed in front of him during the journey to the scaffold. Once there, the same ghastly performance was enacted. Subsequently his head, together with that of

Thomas Harrison, was spiked on top of Westminster Hall, the building in which both men had once practised as barristers.

Many famous men of the day attended the executions, one of them being John Evelyn, the renowned diarist. Late for the executions of regicides Scroope, Scot, Cook and Jones, he nevertheless 'met their quarters mangl'd and cutt and reeking as they were brought from the gallows in baskets on the hurdle'.

Among the lesser known regicides was one John Barkstead who, from a career as a goldsmith in the Strand, became a Roundhead officer and later Governor of Reading. Elected Member of Parliament for Colchester, more honours followed, for on 12 August 1652 Cromwell appointed him Lieutenant of the Tower of London and knighted him four years later.

For Sir John, those times were good. The Tower was full of prisoners, rich Royalist prisoners, and the Lieutenant wasted no time in extorting a vast fortune from his hapless charges in return for such luxuries as extra rations, candles and exercise privileges. But the harvest came to an end in 1660 when the Commonwealth fell, and Sir John hastily fled to the Continent leaving, it was alleged, between £7,000 and £20,000 in gold, sealed in butter firkins and buried in the Tower's cellars. He settled in Germany and became a merchant there, but the vengeful Royalists spread their nets wide to capture and punish the regicides.

The King's Agent in the Netherlands, Sir George Downing (after whom the famous street was named) set a trap to lure Barkstead across the border, under the pretext of a Dutch business deal. Snared, Sir John was brought back to England and imprisoned in the very Tower he had once commanded, and on 16 April 1662 he was hanged and dismembered. As a solemn warning to all, his head was impaled on a pole above Traitors' Gate in the Tower of London. But its lolling tongue kept its secret, for although many have searched, including Samuel Pepys of *Diary* fame, no one is known to have found the Lieutenant's loot. Who knows, perhaps the ancient castle jealously guards *two* prizes of great value, the crown jewels and Barkstead's treasure.

Executioner Dun died on 11 September 1663, his replacement being the infamous Jack Ketch; infamous because, so brutal was his character, so inefficient his performance, that every hangman for decades afterwards was branded, albeit unjustly, with his name, as a mark of public contempt and approbation. Even children were made aware of his infamy for when, in 1702, Punch and Judy shows were introduced into England from Italy, the hangman puppet was promptly christened Jack Ketch.

About the only person who did not share the general condemnation was Jack's loyal wife, for she boasted proudly that 'any bungler could put a man to death, but only her husband knew how to make a gentleman die sweetly'. An opinion not shared by Jack's clients!

Ketch adopted the title of 'Esquire' himself, on the assumption that the arms granted to Gregory Brandon in 1617 applied equally to successive hangmen. Other unofficial titles came his way, his letters frequently being addressed to 'Dr John Ketch at the sign of the Three Legged Stool near Hyde Park Corner' (the Tyburn gallows).

His exploits were of course reported almost daily in the broadsheets, the media of the day. When, in 1678, Titus Oates and others accused prominent Roman Catholics of conspiring to assassinate the King, one of those condemned to death was Edward Coleman, secretary to the Duchess of York. Journalists had a field day, one of them publishing 'The Plotters Ballad, being Jack Ketch's Incomparable Receipt [recipe] for the Cure of Traytorous Recusants, or wholesome Physick for a Popish Contagion'. The broadsheet was illustrated by a woodcut showing Coleman being dragged to his execution on a sledge and exclaiming 'I am sick of a traytorious disease' to which Ketch, brandishing his axe, replies 'Here's your cure, Sir!'

Years later Oates, his accusations having been proved false, was to become Ketch's prey, but not until many innocent heads had rolled, among them those of Lord Stafford and the Catholic Primate of Ireland.

The latter, Oliver Plunket, Archbishop of Armagh, was

convicted at Newgate of conspiring to bring a French army to Ireland, and so condemned to death. He was dragged to Tyburn and there half strangled and mutilated, his heart and entrails being burnt on the scaffold fire.

But while the savage dismembering was taking place, the Archbishop's severed head was surreptitiously removed from the basket and smuggled away through the crowds. It was later sent to Cardinal Howard in Rome, who presented it to Archbishop Hugh McMahon. He brought it to Ireland in 1722, and a visitor to the Dominican convent in Drogheda in the 1920s described how, within a silver and ebony casket, the head lay on a cloth, its skin dried and perfectly preserved, its sparse hair singed from the Tyburn fire. The eyes were closed, the features relaxed in peace and dignity.

After the disembowelling on the scaffold, the body was placed in a coffin and, in accordance with orders from Charles II, was taken to the cemetery of St Giles in the Fields, a church situated near the junction of Oxford Street and Tottenham Court Road, London. There it was buried, the service being read by Father Corker, who had been a fellow prisoner of the Archbishop in Newgate Gaol.

A copper plate buried with the coffin was inscribed:

In this tomb resteth the body of the Right Rev. Oliver Plunket, Archbishop of Armagh and Primate of Ireland, who in hatred of religion was accused of high treason by false witnesses, and for the same condemned and executed at Tyburn the first of July 1681, in the reign of Charles II.

Two years later the remains were exhumed and taken to the Benedictine Abbey of St Adrian at Lamspringe, near Hildesheim, Germany, where they remained until 1803, when they were interred in the graveyard there. Eighty years later the relics were removed to St Gregory's Monastery at Downside, Bath. Prior to the original burial in 1681 Father Corker had had the arms amputated below the elbows and one of these relics was first preserved at Samsfield Court, Herefordshire, but later taken to a Franciscan convent at Taunton in Somerset.

Ketch's bloody career continued as it had started,

although occasionally he had his personal problems. In 1679 he ran up a debt of £22, a considerable sum then, and served a short term of imprisonment in the Marshalsea Prison, a gaol not far from his home in Spreadeagle Alley, near Bow Street, Westminster. And in 1682, as a change from striking with the axe, he struck for more pay, though it is not recorded whether he was successful.

There is little doubt that the duties involved were enough to de-humanize even the most compassionate of men, as evidenced by John Ellwood who was imprisoned in Newgate at that time and who recounted his experiences in his autobiography, which he wrote in 1670. In particular he described the scenes in the room known as 'Jack Ketch's Kitchen':

> a little byplace like a closet neer where we lodged, and in it lay the quartered bodies of three men who had been executed some days before. Their quarters had lain there so long because their relatives were still seeking permission to bury them which at length with much ado was granted. But only for the quarters, not for the heads, which were ordered to be set up in some part of the City. I saw the heads when they were brought up to be boiled; the hangman brought them in a dirty dust basket, out of some place, and setting them down among the felons, he and they made sport of them. They took them by the hair, flouting, jeering and laughing at them; and then, giving them ill names, boxed them on the ears and cheeks. Which done, Ketch put them into his kettle and parboiled them with Bay-salt and Cummin-seed ... the whole night was both frightful and loathsome and begat an abhorrence in my nature.

Early in the eighteenth century another executioner strode the scaffold boards, big and brawny as befitted an ex-blacksmith. His name was William Marvell, and his reign of only two years, though brief, was both eventful and profitable.

Well known in most of the London taverns, he has been described as a grim-looking man, and when Harrison Ainsworth, the Victorian novelist, used him as a character in his book *Jack Sheppard*, Ainsworth said that he was tall and sinister-looking, with harsh, inflexible features, a muscular frame and large, bony hands.

Despite his repellent appearance, Marvell married twice, having three sons by his first wife, though it must be admitted that two of them were later hanged and the third son was transported to the colonies. Marvell himself was no shining example as a father, for by 1706 he had already been convicted twice for theft.

In 1715 the hangman John Price was imprisoned for debt and Marvell was appointed to replace him; his skills as a blacksmith made him well qualified to swing the axe. From Marvell's point of view the job could not have come at a better time, for over the border the first Jacobite Uprising was about to erupt. Scottish lords and their followers swept south, determined to place James Edward Stuart, son of James II, on the English throne, and the clansmen fought their way as far as Preston in Lancashire before being defeated.

Their leaders were taken to the Tower, three of them being condemned to death, the Earl of Nithsdale, Lord Kenmure and the Earl of Derwentwater, even though the last was a grandson of Charles II. The Earl of Nithsdale foiled the headsman by getting away from the Tower dressed as a woman, but for the other two, only the axe awaited.

On the night of the executions the Aurora Borealis shone with unusual brilliance, an omen, it was said, of heaven's wrath, and many Scottish folk ever after referred to the display as 'Lord Derwentwater's Lights'.

As a mark of royal grace the heads were not exhibited on London Bridge but were interred with the bodies. Derwentwater's remains were initially taken to a private Catholic chapel at Dagenham Park near Romford, where his ghost is still said to walk, but later the coffin was transferred to the family vault in Dilston Castle in Northumberland.

In 1805 the vault was opened and the public allowed to view the remains. 'The hair was quite perfect,' wrote the author Richard Davey, 'the features regular and wearing the appearance of youth. The marks of the axe were quite visible and the shroud but little decayed.' Reverence for the dead was not universal, however, for a local blacksmith stole some of the Earl's teeth and sold them at four for £1!

In the 1830s a further search revealed a number of caskets, one of which contained the Earl's heart and other organs. This and the coffin were afterwards sealed up and the mausoleum secured. A decade later, an oak chest was found in a country house at Thorndon in Essex, containing not only the Earl's clothes (minus those claimed by Marvell, of course) but also the cloth which had covered the block, stiffened with the young lord's blood, its fibres split by the one fatal blow of the axe. This, incidentally, is one of the few instances in which, reportedly, the victim's head rested on anything other than the bare wood of the block.

In 1735 the scaffold was ascended by the last hangman to execute by means of the axe, one John Thrift, a simple, uneducated man, temperamentally unsuited to his death-dealing role. Prone to nerves, susceptible to the drama of the moment, he was unsure with the rope, inexpert with the axe and inaccurate with the cleaver, yet for seventeen years he blundered his way through hangings and beheadings until his death in 1752.

His performance on the scaffold improved little over the years, but his capabilities were really put to the test in 1746 when the Scottish clans rose again, in the second Jacobite Uprising. After a series of battles, their defeat brought many prisoners to Thrift's gallows, to be hanged, drawn and quartered.

Among the first batch of Jacobites was Colonel Francis Towneley, a brave and loyal supporter of the Pretender, who had fought against overwhelming odds in many of the battles, and showed no less courage and steadfastness on the scaffold. His ordeal at Thrift's hands was described in the relevant *State Trials*:

After he had hung six minutes, he was cut down and, having life in him, as he lay on the block to be quartered, the executioner gave him several blows to his breast, which not having the effect designed, he immediately cut his throat; after which he took his head off, then ripped him open and took out his bowels and heart and threw them in a fire which consumed them. Then he slashed his four quarters and put them with the head into a coffin, and they were carried to the new gaol at Southwark, and on 2 August the head was put on Temple Bar and his body and limbs suffered to be buried.

Temple Bar, which once straddled Fleet Street as a boundary between the City of London and the City of Westminster, was a high ornamental stone archway designed by Sir Christopher Wren in 1673 to replace an earlier wooden structure. It had received its first trophy in 1683 when Sir Thomas Armstrong, found guilty of treason, involuntarily donated one of his quarters to be exhibited thereon.

His other quarters were placed on Aldgate and Aldersgate in the City, the fourth quarter being sent to intimidate his erstwhile supporters in his former constituency of Stafford. And for many years Sir Thomas's head graced the roof of Westminster Hall, until the skull finally disintegrated.

Later remains on Temple Bar included the heads of two would-be assassins of William III, Sir John Friend and Sir William Perkins, in 1696. And in 1723 Christopher Layer, a barrister involved in a Jacobite conspiracy to capture the Tower and imprison the King and the Prince of Wales, was also granted the privilege of a bird's-eye view of Fleet Street. For more than thirty years his head was a fixture on Temple Bar until one stormy night it fell down and rolled into the Strand. When found, it was given to a local innkeeper who buried it beneath the wooden floor of his tavern.

Layer's head was still in place however when, in 1746, it was joined by those of Towneley and a fellow Jacobite, George Fletcher. In such a crowded thoroughfare as Fleet Street, public interest was intense, illustrated posters being distributed and broadsheet ballads being sold, all applauding the traitors' fate. Horace Walpole, *en route* to the Tower, described how 'while passing under the new heads at Temple Bar, I saw people making a trade of letting spy glasses at a halfpenny a look'.

The heads of Towneley and Fletcher remained until 1772, the last to be exhibited there, although their survival was threatened on 20 January 1766 when, as recorded in the *Annual Register*, a man was charged with having, at 2.30 a.m., discharged musket balls from a crossbow at the two heads. In defence he stated that in his opinion the punishment already inflicted on the traitors was not sufficient, and not only had he peppered them with shot on the previous three nights, but he intended to continue, using the fifty musket balls found in his possession.

On 1 April 1772 one head fell down, followed shortly by the other. The descent of such grim relics from city gates never failed to cause havoc among passers-by, for it was one thing to view a head at a distance, but quite another when 'the black, shapeless lump fell. Women screamed, men gasped in horror. One woman near me fainted at the sight' recalled the wife of the editor of the contemporary *Morning Chronicle*.

For information on the fate of Colonel Towneley's head I am indebted to Susan Bourne, curator of Towneley Hall, Burnley. Once the family home, it is now a splendid art gallery and museum. When, in 1772, the gallant soldier's head fell, it was claimed by a family retainer and brought home to the Hall. There it was kept for many years in the red drawing room, in a large basket covered with a napkin. It was later deposited behind oak panelling in the family chapel but, being adjacent to hot-water pipes, the hair remaining became crinkled and the skull and teeth blackened.

When retrieved, the head was sealed in a glass box and placed reverently beneath the altar and, later, on 12 August 1947, it was interred in the tomb within the Towneley Chapel in St Peter's Parish Church, Burnley, a final and fitting resting-place for a brave and loyal soldier.

Colonel Towneley's leaders in the 1745 rebellion were the Earl of Kilmarnock, Lord Balmerino and Simon, Lord Lovat. Lovat had previously petitioned the King, wrote James Ray in his book: 'that he may be executed after the manner of the Scots nobility i.e. by an Engine called the Maiden, which falls with great Velocity and at one blow severs the Head from the Body' (a device described later in the chapter 'Grandees of the Guillotine'). But His Majesty rejected the appeal and so Lord Lovat has the dubious honour of being the last man to die by the axe in England.

On 8 April 1747, after an early glass of wine and water, Lovat had a good breakfast of minced veal, and ordered coffee and chocolate for his friends with him in the Tower. Taken to Tower Hill at 11 a.m., he accepted a drink of burnt brandy and bitters from the sheriff and was then assisted to the scaffold by two Tower warders. On seeing the enormous crowd, some people even clinging to masts of ships moored in the river, he exclaimed 'God save us! Why should there be such a hustle about taking off an old grey head that can't even get up three steps without three bodies to support it?'

The crush was so great that a grandstand collapsed, killing twenty spectators and injuring many more. Among those who lost their lives were the carpenter who had erected the stand, and his wife who had been selling liquor beneath it.

After checking the edge of the axe held by Thrift, Lovat gave the executioner ten guineas in lieu of his gold-headed cane, hat, wig and clothes which he bequeathed to his Scottish agent. His two yeoman warders assisted him to kneel – he was after all an old man of eighty years – but Thrift, anxious to be accurate, required him to move back a little. This Lovat did, and while the onlookers watched breathlessly, down thundered the axe as John Thrift redeemed himself, removing the grey head at a single stroke.

Rather than allow the head to roll on to the boards, it was caught in a white cloth held by two men and, with the body, placed in the waiting coffin. Later, witnessed by George Selwyn, a fashionable wit and politician who regularly attended executions, the head was sewn back on to the body, and plans for the burial were initiated.

State Papers Domestic of April 1747 quotes Lord Lovat's instructions to his cousin William Fraser:

that you will order my Body be carefully put up in a lead coffin after my execution and there to be preserved and transported to the House of Muniack where the same is to lay for a night or Two and then interr'd under my own Tomb in the Church of Kirkhill, and as soon as the corpse arrive at Inverness you are to order any two of my Friends you think proper to invite so many of my friends and relations as you in consert with others shall advice to attend my Funeral.

So William Fraser and another relative James Fraser, escorted the coffin back to the Tower, there to wait until the immense crowds had dispersed. When the public execution site had quietened down, Stevenson, an undertaker acting on the Frasers' orders, collected the coffin and took it to his funeral parlour in the Strand where, reaping the benefits of the day's great event in the City, promptly charged admission for the public to view the corpse.

When news of this scandalous exhibition reached the authorities – 'the great indignity as well as the indecencie of it, a thing never before heard of', as James Ray quotes – William Fraser was told not to take the coffin north to Scotland, despite the fact that he had arranged for Hugh Inglis, master of the good ship *The Pledger*, then moored in the Thames, to collect and transport it there. And the Cabinet decided that Lord Lovat's remains should instead be buried within the Tower of London.

But here the plot thickens. While all these negotiations were going on, the corpse, removed from public display had, in accordance with Lord Lovat's wishes, been placed in a lead coffin and its lid soldered down. And eight days after the execution the corpse was duly interred in the Chapel Royal of St Peter, within the Tower, where it remains to this very day. Or does it?

In a letter to *Notes and Queries* of December 1884, a descendant, Sir William Fraser, claimed that Lovat's body and head were taken by night to Kirkhill, near Inverness, and that a few weeks before writing his letter he had actually seen the lead coffin containing the remains. Moreover there is a strong local tradition that the head (if nothing else) was in a tin box deposited in the family vault, but that the box had since disappeared.

So, as the authorities had collected the sealed coffin from the London undertaker without question or examination, were the remains of Simon, Lord Lovat really spirited away to his native country? And is the lead coffin, buried originally at the west end of the Chapel Royal and re-interred with others in its crypt in 1876, empty?

Many victims of the scaffold, whether Jesuit priests or fervent patriots, had their loyal sympathizers, and Simon Fraser, Lord Lovat, was no exception. In 1914, long before most exhibits in the Tower were encased behind glass to protect them from the public, a young woman was caught digging her fingernails into the axe-riven block on display, reputedly the very one on which Lovat's head had been severed. When questioned she disclosed that she and others had obtained blood-stained splinters in this way, preserving them in lockets for remembrance.

Although Lord Lovat was the last man to be executed by the axe, he was not the last man to be beheaded by one! That claim to fame goes to three men, Jeremiah Brandreth, William Turner and Isaac Ludlam, who were accused of leading riots in the Derbyshire insurrection of 1817, a year of social unrest and distress in the country. Most of the rioters were transported to the colonies but the three leaders were sentenced to be hanged, drawn and quartered at Derby, the penalty being reduced to one of being hanged and beheaded after death, with no other mutilation taking place.

The suggestion that a knife be used was rejected by the Prince Regent, who insisted on the axe! For reasons unknown, the Tower axe was not sent for. Instead a local blacksmith made two identical copies of the Tower original, and a gallows was constructed outside Derby gaol.

A vast crowd had assembled, sympathizers being kept back from the scaffold by cavalry and soldiers. The three victims were led out and were duly hanged, their bodies being left on the rope for almost an hour. Jeremiah Brandreth's body was cut down first and placed face down on a long trestle which had a neck support nailed to one end. An anonymous local miner, masked for the occasion, swung the axe, but even two blows were insufficient, and an assistant had to complete the severance with a knife.

Playing the part to the full, the 'executioner' then lifted the head high; whereupon the crowd, overcome with horror at the ghastly spectacle, fled from the scene. The grisly drama was re-enacted, with the corpses of Turner and Ludlam being similarly mutilated. The crowd's aversion to the scene, in contrast to those who relished such spectacles a century or more earlier, was perhaps indicative of the public's increasing social awareness and sensitivity. And the poet Shelley, who was present at the Derby executions, angrily petitioned the authorities against ever repeating such nauseating events.

But repeat it they did, thankfully for the last time. The continuing depression of the early 1800s bred more discontent, this time in London, where similar-minded conspirators planned riot and revolution, as usual to include the massacre of Cabinet ministers and the seizing of the Tower and Bank of England.

The ringleader was Arthur Thistlewood, a man who had instigated the Spafields riot a year earlier, for which a fellow conspirator was hanged. Thistlewood, a great admirer of Robespierre, the French revolutionary, was a gambler, a spendthrift and a born agitator. Believing that only force would bring about his brand of rabid socialism, he recruited similarly minded men to his cause. John Brunt and Richard Tidd were cobblers, James Ings a butcher, and these four, together with a coloured man, William Davidson, formed the notorious Cato Street Conspiracy.

Their plan was nothing if not audacious. Having learned the date on which nearly all the Cabinet ministers would be dining with Lord Harrowby at his house in Grosvenor Square, they intended to burst in and massacre the entire assembly. Then, heavily armed, they would seize the Mansion House and Bank of England, and gain complete mastery of the City by taking over the Tower of London.

Such a plot verged on utter fantasy, yet their deadly intention to wipe out most of the government could well have succeeded had not another member of the gang been an undercover agent who was keeping the authorities advised of every move.

When information came of the gang's final meeting, the law went into action, police cornering them in a house in Cato Street (now renamed Homer Street) near the Edgware Road, in London. All were arrested, charged with high treason and, on 3 March 1820 they achieved one of their ambitions, to enter the Tower of London. Not exactly in the way they would have wished, however.

Thistlewood, appropriately enough, was imprisoned in the Bloody Tower, Ings and Davidson in St Thomas's Tower above Traitors' Gate, Brunt in the Byward Tower and Tidd in a fortified area of the outer battlemented wall, near to where the author of this book recently resided.

Having been tried and found guilty, they were taken to Newgate on 1 May, for execution. The condemned men were far from penitent, and treated the scaffold as a stage from which to entertain their many supporters in the vast crowd. Some of the five felons sucked oranges; Tidd danced a jig and Ings sang 'Death or Liberty' twice, while Thistlewood himself theatrically proclaimed 'We shall soon know the great secret!'

James Botting, the hangman, did not begrudge the crowd their moments of hero worship but then, as St Sepulchre's bell struck eight o'clock, the ropes were tightened, the drop operated. The vocalist Ings alone caused trouble, kicking and squirming so that Botting and his assistant Foxen pulled on a leg each; little more than five minutes elapsed before death ensued.

Their crime having been treason, the penalty was that they should be hanged, drawn and quartered. As in the Derbyshire case, this too was mitigated to one of being hanged and beheaded after death, the last time such a sentence has been carried out in England.

After hanging for an hour, while the crowd waited, noisy and impatient, the bodies were cut down. Coffins lay in readiness on the scaffold and the bodies were placed in them so that each head protruded over the side, to rest on a high wooden block. It was then that a masked man, alleged to be a surgeon, appeared, to decapitate each corpse with a knife, giving the heads to Botting. And each one in turn was raised high by the hangman as, striving to make himself heard above the deafening chorus of jeers and abuse from the seething mob around the scaffold, he loudly proclaimed 'This is the head of a traitor!'

As the heads were put with the bodies in the coffins, the crowd erupted into violence, and Botting and assistant Foxen had to flee for their lives behind the massive gates of the gaol. When eventually the mob had dispersed, the coffins were buried within the prison confines.

And with the execution of the Cato Street Conspirators, the reign of the heading axe, the cleaver and decapitating knife, the boiling cauldron and blazing scaffold fire, was finally at an end.

2   Slayers with the Sword

The Central Criminal Court, the Old Bailey, is situated in the heart of the City of London. Its copper dome is surmounted by a bronze statue of Justice, sixteen feet high, holding in her left hand the scales, to emphasize the balance with which all evidence will be weighed. In her right hand she grasps the symbol of retribution administered to those found guilty, the Sword of Justice.

Yet by rights this symbol should be a hempen noose or an axe, for it would seem that on only one occasion since the days of the Norman kings has a sword been officially used for an execution in England – for the beheading of Queen Anne Boleyn, within the Tower of London.

Charged with adultery and treason, she had been sentenced 'to be burnt alive or beheaded, at the King's pleasure' and His Majesty had granted her the unusual privilege of being decapitated by the sword, a method infinitely preferable to suffering death by the brutal axe.

And so it was, on 19 May 1536, that she was led on to Tower Green with an escort of 200 Yeomen of the Guard, through the massed ranks of spectators, noblemen of the Court, aldermen of the City of London, officers of the Tower.

The Queen wore a loose robe of grey damask over a red underskirt, the robe having a deep white collar furred with ermine. Her long black hair, beneath a white coif, was further concealed by a small black cap. At her girdle hung a gold chain and cross, and she carried a handkerchief and a little prayer book bound in gold.

On the Green the scaffold had been erected. 'Send at once to Master Eretage for carpenters to make a scaffold of such a height that all present may see it,' wrote Sir William Kingston, Constable of the Tower. Accordingly it stood five feet high, surrounded by a low rail and of course covered with straw.

Sir William assisted the Queen to mount the steps of the scaffold, where the executioner awaited. As there was no English headsman capable of wielding a sword for such a purpose, one had been brought over from Calais (still an English possession). The Frenchman was a terrifying figure, clad in a tight-fitting black suit, a half mask of the same colour covering the upper part of his face, and a high, horn-shaped cap on his head. This grim uniform, new for the occasion, had been paid for by the Constable of the Tower, the Record Office accounts showing that Sir William received one hundred crowns in French money 'to give to the executioner of Calays for his rewarde and apparail'.

After prayers and a short speech in which she declared her innocence and loyalty to the King, Anne's cape was removed and, taking off both black cap and coif, she replaced them with a white linen cap. The Queen knelt again, as did most of the spectators, and as their prayers ended Mistress Lee, her lady-in-waiting, bound her eyes with a linen handkerchief.

The headsman, considerate enough to have hidden his sword beneath the straw, then signalled his English assistant to approach the Queen, thereby distracting her attention. As she turned her head slightly the executioner seized his opportunity. Grasping the sword he swung and, with one blow, severed her head.

Instantly, blood gushed over the scaffold boards, and several women onlookers fainted as he held the head high, horror mounting as the eyes and lips were seen to open and close convulsively.

The historian Crispin, who wrote an account of the scene two weeks after her death, described how

her ladies immediately took up her head and the body. They were so languid and extremely weak within anguish, but fearing that their mistress might be handled unworthily by inhuman men, they forced themselves to do this duty, and at last carried off her dead body wrapt in a white covering.

No coffin having been provided, it is reported that a yeoman warder obtained an old arrow-chest made of elm wood, in which the corpse was placed. Incidentally, the story that such a makeshift coffin was utilized lends some credence to the irreverent music-hall song, 'With her head tucked underneath her arm'. An arrow-chest, being shorter than a coffin, would leave insufficient space for the head to be placed on the shoulders, and it would be logical therefore to place it in the crook of one arm.

In the Chapel Royal of St Peter ad Vincula a blessing was pronounced over the rude coffin, which was then buried under the altar near that of her brother George, Lord Rochford.

In 1876, by command of Queen Victoria, a committee was formed, to supervise the exhumation and possible identification of all those interred in the chapel; bodies of those who, like Sir Thomas More and many others, were executed on Tower Hill and had been buried in the nave, the absence of their heads and the callous method of their burial making identification impossible. All such remains were accordingly reverently re-interred in the crypt.

Excavations beneath the altar uncovered the remains of a young female having 'a well formed round skull, intellectual forehead, straight orbital ridge, large eyes and a square full chin', as described by one of those present, Mr Doyne Bell.

From these characteristics, and the small vertebrae discovered (evidence of the Queen's 'lyttel neck'), the remains were identified by Mr Mouat, a surgical expert, as being 'all consistent with public descriptions of Queen Anne Boleyn, and the bones of the skull might well belong to the person portrayed in Holbein's painting of the Queen'.

The remains, and those of others reported buried there, namely Queen Catherine Howard, the Duke of Northumberland, the Countess of Salisbury, Lord Rochford, the latter's wife Lady Rochford, and the Duke of Somerset, were re-interred, being individually placed in thick leaden coffins. Their covers were soldered down and they were then deposited in boxes of oak plank one inch thick, the lids of which were secured with copper screws.

Each box bore a leaden escutcheon with the name of the person supposedly enclosed, and all were buried four inches below the surface of the altar. The area was then concreted and overlaid with green, red and white mosaic marble, the designs having borders of yellow Sienna marble, and bearing the names and crests of some of the victims.

The severing of Queen Anne's head with a single stroke pays tribute to the skill of French executioners who, until the adoption of the guillotine in 1792, meted out death by the sword to those of the upper classes who had been sentenced to death.

The sword of the renowned French executioner Charles-Henri Sanson, of whom more in a later chapter, was engraved on one side of the blade with the word '*Justicia*', and with the wheel, the emblem of torture, on the other side and, being designed specifically for its task, was a superbly balanced weapon.

Sanson, conscientious as he was, woefully lacked accuracy in his early days but, by practising on straw dummies, soon achieved the skill he demonstrated when executing the Chevalier de la Barre. In 1766 the guardian of a wealthy girl had plans for her marriage but she preferred another, the handsome, nineteen-year-old Chevalier. Her guardian, the Lieutenant Criminel of Abbeville, accused the Chevalier of failing to salute some passing monks, an irreligious act warranting execution.

Sanson was sent for and on the scaffold the Chevalier was told to kneel. Upon his refusal Sanson protested:

'But it is the custom for criminals to kneel.'

'I am no criminal,' the Chevalier retorted. 'Do your duty. I shall give you no trouble, only be quick.'

Raising the sword, Sanson swung it and struck with such accuracy that the severed head remained balanced on the upright body for a few seconds. And true or not, witnesses say they heard Sanson exclaim 'Shake yourself – it's done!'

By now it should be apparent that no block was used in conjunction with the sword. Indeed it would be almost impossible, for the edge of the blade would first encounter the side of the block before striking the victim's neck, unless the executioner also knelt, and that position would prevent him from giving sufficient impetus to the blade to sever the head.

The procedure therefore was that the victim, after baring his or her neck, would kneel and, for their own sakes, remain absolutely motionless. This position brought the target to an ideal level for the executioner to aim the sword accurately, sometimes swinging it two or three times to gain momentum before striking horizontally.

No executioner was infallible, of course, even with such a precise weapon. An ancestor of Charles-Henri, called upon to execute Angelique Tiquet in 1699 for planning the murder of her husband, failed abysmally. 'Kneel down with your head up and your hair lifted off your neck and falling over your face,' he instructed. Yet at the last moment the sword swerved, slicing her ear and cheek. The impact propelled her forward and two assistants had to hold her, two more strokes of the sword being necessary to decapitate her.

Even the great Charles-Henri's aim went astray occasionally. When beheading the Comte de Lally-Tollendal in 1766, the blade cut into the victim's jaw and cheek, breaking his teeth. Quickly an assistant seized the Comte, holding him by the ears, and Charles-Henri's elderly father, Jean-Baptiste, took the sword and unerringly removed the victim's head.

Amateurs there were of course, men who volunteered for the job in order to save their own skins, and it was one of these who, in 1626, took twenty-nine strokes of the sword to end the life of the Comte de Chalais.

Across the border, German executioners also had superb weapons of precision at their disposal, two of which are in the Royal Armouries at the Tower of London.

One, dating from about 1602, has a fig-shaped pommel and a button of gilt brass, and still retains the original leather on its two-handed grip. The blade itself, two inches wide and thirty-one inches long, has a broad, blunt tip, no point being necessary. The sword weighs four pounds one ounce, its overall length being thirty-nine and a half inches, and it was made by Clemens Keuller, a swordsmith of the early seventeenth century.

The other execution sword was made about the year 1700. A rather longer one, it measures forty-three and a half inches overall, its blade being two and a half inches wide and thirty-four and a quarter inches long. Weighing four pounds, it has survived the centuries well, still bearing traces of gilding on the brass hilt. The quillons (guards) are straight and the two-handed grip is still covered with fish skin. As befits its purpose, the sharpened edges of its blade are parallel, and its tip rounded.

Near the grip, on each side, is a 'fuller', a wide groove cut longitudinally into the blade. Bordering the grooves are etched floral decorations, a grim motto being inscribed in each of the wide grooves. On the obverse, the words 'Wan Ich Dass Schwert thue auffheben, So Wünsche Ich dem süncler das E. Ieben' (whenever I raise the sword, I wish the sinner everlasting life). Next to it is a finely detailed engraving of a wheel, symbolizing an earlier, more barbaric method of execution.

On the reverse of the blade appear the words 'Die Herren Steüren Dem Unheill, Ich Execuirire Iht Ends Urtheill' (the judges check evil, I carry out their capital judgement), and next to it is engraved the gallows.

The German executioner was the *Scharfrichter*, known colloquially as the 'Mate of Death', and his assistant was the *Löwe*, the Lion, the name apparently being derived from the roars he emitted when dragging the prisoner in front of the judge. In addition to assisting the executioner he was the city council's jack of all trades. He was responsible for clearing the market square of rubbish, quelling hooligans, burying unclaimed corpses, burning the bodies of suicides, branding criminals; an invaluable man to have on the town's payroll.

At executions he it was who carried the pall and the keys to the scaffold enclosure and, should the sentence be one of drowning, he had the job of pushing the felon, who was tied in a sack, under the surface using a long pole.

On the scaffold the *Löwe* ran considerable risks, literally taking his life into his hands, for should he be required to support the victim, an ill-considered positioning of his own body or limbs, or an ill-judged swing of the sword, could result in instant amputation or worse. The *Löwe* assisting executioner Johann Widman in 1717 nearly lost both hands when the victim flinched at the last moment.

Such was the momentum of the heavy sword in the hands of an experienced executioner that on 20 October 1645 Master Matthias Perger not only took off the felon's head but, the victim having raised his hands, severed them as well. And another executioner earned the crowd's ecstatic applause when he beheaded two criminals with one blow!

As in England, bodies of traitors were quartered and exhibited on the city gates. And not only were women put to the sword but the heads of those guilty of child murder were nailed above the gallows.

A terrifying warning was occasionally administered in cases where extenuating circumstances existed. The prisoner would endure a mock execution – the macabre procession, the prayers and scaffold formalities, even to having the noose placed in position or the sword swung above his or her head: a nightmare experience whether the victim was informed in advance or not.

Perhaps the most renowned of Germany's executioners was Franz Schmidt who bestrode Nuremberg's scaffold from 1573 to 1617. No record of his early life has survived but it is known that his father was executioner of the German town of Bamberg. Franz was his assistant there from 1573 to 1578 and when thoroughly proficient he moved to Nuremberg, where he became chief executioner. Franz's skill with the various tools of his trade was due in no small part to his interest in anatomy, knowledge of which he put to further use in the dissection of some of his victims. Hospitals were always in need of specimens for medical research and it was the hangman's duty in most countries to supply them.

Not that he was inhumane, on the contrary, for in 1580 he used his influence to have the penalty of drowning, which was inflicted on women guilty of infanticide, changed to the more merciful one of hanging or beheading.

As in England, Germany's public executioners were feared and loathed by the populace and this included their assistants, but despite society's rejection Franz performed his duties with impersonal efficiency and dedication. Unlike many of his calling he never drank strong liquor, and such had been his upbringing that his ability to write encouraged him to keep a detailed diary of his official activities, annotated accordingly where the felon had finally confessed his misdeeds.

A contemporary picture portrays Schmidt as a tall well-built man, full bearded, in jerkin and knee-length hose. He could afford to dress well for the pay was good. He received a fixed salary, with an extra fee per execution and half that sum for each felon tortured. He and his assistant were also loaned to neighbouring authorities whenever they lacked an executioner of their own, and a higher rate was then paid. The team even received some compensation in the event of a last-minute reprieve being granted to the condemned person.

Nor did Franz have any rent to pay, for he occupied an official residence provided by the city council, a tower house on the stone bridge which straddled Nuremberg's River Pegnitz.

Like their English counterparts, German executioners did a good trade in providing the superstitious with severed portions of their victims' corpses for use as revered relics, medicines or lucky charms. However, care had to be taken to ensure that such relics were not purchased for illicit purposes.

In those days a macabre belief existed among the criminal fraternity of Europe that the severed hand of a hanged man, if prepared in accordance with the ancient recipes, possessed special powers. This unpleasant relic was called the Hand of Glory and in order to achieve its magical function it had first to be converted into a gruesome candlestick. To this end, several formulae existed. One stipulated that the right hand be severed before the flesh had withered away, and it then had to be drained of blood. Wrapped in a winding sheet, it was next placed in a pot containing dragon-wort before being bleached in the sun till the marrow melted.

Following that stage, a candle made of murderer's fat and Lapland sesame had to be made, its wick being of a corpse's twisted hair or of fibres from a hangman's rope. The fingers of the hand having been bent towards the palm, the candle was then inserted either between the two middle fingers, the hand thereby being held upright in use, or in the middle of the palm after the fashion of a conventional candlestick.

Another prescription called for the hand to be drained of blood and dried in a pot containing salt and saltpetre, to dry and mummify it. After being subsequently baked in an oven fuelled with fern and vervain, a herb used as a powerful charm, the fingers and thumb of the hand were each threaded with a wick made from five locks of the dead man's hair soaked in a mixture of fat from his body and that of a black tom cat. The final ingredient was the reciting of the Lord's Prayer, backwards.

Once the wicks were lighted, the blazing Hand of Glory would be carried into the house being burgled, its powers either rendering its holder invisible, or causing the occupants of the house to fall into trancelike slumber. Other evil-doers believed that the Hand would indicate what best to steal, by extinguishing its own light when above the place where the valuables were hidden.

It was also believed that similar magical properties were possessed by suitably modified fingers of unborn babies, and so pregnant women ran the terrible risk of being murdered and mutilated in order to obtain these ghastly candles. Such human artifacts were much sought after, mention of them even being made in Shakespeare's play *Macbeth*, in which the witches' cauldron was said to contain, among other ingredients, the finger of a birth-strangled baby.

In Germany such horrific crimes were effectively dealt with by Franz Schmidt, one instance being the murder and mutilation of five women by a criminal Bastion Grubl, who was hanged at Nuremberg on 21 April 1601.

A German executioner's duties did not start on the scaffold, of course, but in the cells beneath the courtroom. There the executioner and his assistant would endeavour to coax a confession from the accused, utilizing the several instruments of torture provided by the authorities. If the thumbscrews didn't persuade, the 'ladder' might, stretching the bound victim to an agonizing degree. There was the 'fass', a spiked cradle in which the victim was tied and then rocked violently, or the 'gauntlets' whereby the accused, hands bound behind him, was hoisted aloft by the wrists, weights then being attached to his ankles.

On the day of the trial Franz would knock on the door of the cell, formally apologize and, having tied the prisoner's wrists, would drape a white cloak around the felon's shoulders and lead him to the courtroom for judgement. After sentence had been duly passed the felon, led by two mounted constables, would be taken in a cart, accompanied by two chaplains. The assistant executioner followed with the coffin, and also bearing a flagon of strong drink with which to fortify the victim for his or her coming ordeal.

Outside the city gate the grim procession would halt for the sacrament to be administered, before proceeding to the scaffold through the vast crowds gathered to watch the execution. On arrival at the scaffold the *Löwe* would read out a proclamation warning of the punishment that waited anyone attempting to impede or avenge the coming execution.

There were two scaffold sites in old Nuremberg, the Hochgericht, the high gallows, and the Rabenstein, the ravens' stone. The latter was so called because of the many ravens which in early times nested in the surrounding trees, its name being an interesting parallel to the Tower of London's birds of ill-omen.

Both sites had massive bases of stone so that all could get a good view, and on execution day the crowds resembled those which gathered at Tyburn and Tower Hill, the German public thronging the square, regaling themselves at the drinking booths, abusing any official in sight but always ready to applaud an efficient performance by Schmidt and his assistants.

And there were certainly many of these. As Franz entered in his diary in 1576: 'Hans Payhel, who committed three murders; two years ago I cut off his ears and flogged him; today I beheaded him at Forcheim.'

On 6 August 1579 he also beheaded three thieves, Büchner, Gabler and Dieterich, an event which came as a considerable shock to Frau Dieterich, for as they were being led out she 'wanted to see the poor sinners, and saw her own husband among them, whom she embraced and kissed, for she had not known her husband had been arrested, nor that he was a fellow of that sort'. What a tragic disillusionment!

There were fellows of another sort in Nuremberg, especially on 10 August 1581. 'George Schörpff, a lecher, guilty of beastliness with four cows, two calves and a sheep, was beheaded for unnatural vice, and was afterwards burnt, together with a cow.' Why the unfortunate animal should be punished was not explained.

Burning after beheading was a practice for which German executioners had to be prepared. Anna Bischoffin, having been whipped out of Würzburg and branded on both cheeks, later set fire to a farm and was beheaded by Schmidt who afterwards burned her body and set her head up on the scaffold. She had hoped to be reprieved by claiming to be pregnant, but the excuse was not accepted.

And anyone who thought that promiscuity should not be punished might care to ponder the fate of Anna Peyelstainin, a client of Franz Schmidt 'because she had carnal intercourse with a father and son, both of whom were married, she also having a husband, and similarly with twenty-one married men and youths, her husband conniving. She was beheaded by the sword, standing, and her husband whipped out of town.'

Of course some people could not be hanged, due to some physical deformity. Agnes Rossnerin, who smothered and throttled her companion in order to steal some money, was beheaded by the sword 'because she was a poor creature and had a wry neck'.

Traitors in any country received short shrift and Hans Ramsperger could hardly complain about the punishment he received on 28 May 1588. Found guilty of being an informer and betraying the city of Nuremberg by revealing where the walls were weakest and most easily stormed, he was beheaded, his body quartered and fixed on the four corners of the scaffold, while his head was spiked on a pole above.

Getting rid of one's spouse was also frowned on in the city. Barbara Wagnerin, wishing to dispose of her husband Lienhardt in order to marry one Conrad Zwickel, administered porridge flavoured with insect powder to Lienhardt. To allay suspicion she ate three spoonfuls herself but was found out. And when the court discovered that she had had immoral relations with eighteen married men and bachelors, they arranged an appointment for her with Franz, who beheaded her with the sword 'as a favour' instead of hanging her.

Such disgraceful goings-on must have filled columns in the tabloids of the day, none more so than those of Andrew Feverstein who kept a school with his father. Having debauched sixteen schoolgirls, he too was granted a 'favour' by Franz, his head being severed on 23 June 1612.

Refinements were also available, such as those given to the servant of Mistress von Ploben. For attacking and killing her mistress, the maid was taken in the cart to the scaffold where, as the snow swirled around them, Franz 'twice nipped her with red-hot tongs' in each arm. Then her head was struck off and fixed on gallows and her body thrown into the pit.

Schmidt served honourably during his forty-four years in office and executed no fewer than 360 felons, at least forty-two of whom were women. His busiest year was 1580, when he performed twenty executions; two were murderers who had to be broken on the wheel, two other murderers and nine thieves being hanged. All of which Franz performed with his usual expertise.

Such was his prowess with the sword that sometimes the speed of the razor-sharp blade left the nerves and facial muscles of the victim still active for minutes after the head had been severed. And he doubtless added to his knowledge of anatomy when he wrote how, after he had decapitated George Praun for robbery on 14 September 1602, 'when placed on the stone the head turned several times as if it wanted to look about it, moved its tongue and opened its mouth as if it wanted to speak, for a good half quarter of an hour. I have never seen the like of this'.

Despite grisly episodes such as these, Franz's career was not entirely humourless. There were always characters like Hans Ditz, pickpocket and murderer who, destined for the sword, sang all the way to the scaffold. And the horse-thief Hans Porstner who, ever the optimist, offered to give the assistant hangman a pair of shoes and five florins if he would change places with him. As the bribe would hardly benefit a dead man, not surprisingly the offer was refused.

There were of course occasions when Franz's great sword was laid aside, other instruments being required for the administration of justice. So it was on 10 January 1583 that three young prostitutes were pilloried and then flogged out of town. One of the unfortunate girls, Mary Kurssnerin, was subsequently caught stealing and so joined Franz on the scaffold. There, after her ears had been cut off, a noose was placed about her neck and she was hanged. Blasphemy was also a crime and when, in 1591, Andrew Brunner was convicted of blaming the Almighty for the severity of a thunderstorm, he was appropriately punished by having a piece of his tongue torn out by Schmidt, who then secured him in the gibbet for the abuse of the crowd.

Many such criminals received their due deserts at the hands of Franz Schmidt, floggings, brandings, amputation of fingers and ears, until finally, in 1617, he decided to retire and become a 'respectable' person again.

He lived quietly in Nuremberg for a further seventeen

years until his death in 1634. The old executioner was given an honourable funeral, the burial service being attended by many of the city dignitaries as a mark of respect for his services to the community.

Not that all German executioners were as honest and expert as Franz, of course. One, Meister Friedrich, manufactured counterfeit coins as a sideline to his scaffold duties and, duly caught, was burned alive at Windsheim in 1386. Another erring headsman, Meister Hans, guilty of treason, suffered the indignity of being decapitated by his own assistant in 1479.

And when it came to sheer incompetence, a prime example was executioner Valtin Deusser, whose blundering performances in 1641 was reported in the Bamberg records:

> the poor sinner was so weak and ill, so that she had to be led to the scaffold and when she sat down upon the chair, Master Valtin the hangman walked round her like a cat round a hot broth and held the sword a span from her neck and took aim and then struck the blow and missed her neck and struck off a piece of her head as big as a dollar and struck her down from the chair. Then the poor soul got up quicker than she had sat down, and this blow did not harm her.
>
> Then she began to beg that she should be allowed to go, because she had been so brave, but all in vain, and she had to sit down again. Then the assistant wanted to take the sword from Master Valtin and strike with it himself, but this the master would not allow, and himself struck a second blow somewhat stronger, so that she again fell to the ground and then he cut her head off as she lay upon the scaffold. Whereupon he, the hangman, had his reward as he went home, for he would soon have been stoned to death if the armed town guard had not rescued him, inasmuch as the blood was already streaming from his head.

As will be apparent from that account, some victims, particularly women, were allowed to sit in a chair if necessary, and one such chair was displayed in Nuremberg in recent years. Other women, and men of short stature, were allowed to stand, rather than kneel to be beheaded.

Because primitive execution by the sword depended so much on the ability or willingness of the victim to remain motionless and unflinching, and also on the dexterity and accuracy of the executioner, the method was eventually phased out. The public spectacle of the decapitation, the headless corpse and gushing blood, became so abhorrent to society that Germany, like many other European countries, adopted the system of hanging its criminals behind prison walls, and the fearsome, blunt-tipped execution swords were honourably retired to museums.

3   Grandees of the Guillotine

If the laws are such that a person must die for the crime he
or she has committed, surely the most instantaneous and
therefore the most merciful method is death by means of
the guillotine. Execution by hanging is always open to
doubt, the timespan between initial strangulation and
final oblivion not being known. The sword and the axe
allow too much leeway for the victim to flinch or the
executioner to mis-aim. And even the multi-executioners
of a firing squad cannot guarantee that at least one bullet
will penetrate the heart. Most other methods are similarly
flawed, whether they are by garotting, gas poisoning,
electric chair or whatever. In other words, there is nothing
so instantly final as a head severed by a machine.

If capital punishment is ever re-adopted, it must
certainly be feasible in this technologically advanced age
to devise an electronically operated guillotine for the
purpose. Similar machines are even now used for many
cutting purposes in industry and could easily be adapted.
Yet for some reason modern society shrinks from such a
method, the objection seeming to be the thought, or sight,
of the resultant blood and the mutilated corpse.

Yet if the victim has died instantaneously and without
suffering, this should be the criterion, and the subsequent
spectacle should not matter. It could easily be resolved
anyway, by modifying the guillotine so that the victim was
accurately positioned in an enclosed container, the lid
incorporating a slot for the blade's entrance. Instruments
would register the completeness of decapitation and the
expiry of life, and the container would then serve the
purpose of the coffin.

I have not patented the method, seeing little chance of it being adopted by a society which, although revelling in violence and bloodshed on the television, is nevertheless squeamish when it comes to punishing adequately those who don't hesitate to inflict mutilation and death on others.

The word guillotine immediately conjures up thoughts of France in general and Paris in particular, but early mention of devices resembling the guillotine occur in Roman literature, and also in Italy, Germany and France itself, the last being reported by a French diarist in 1652 as being 'a mechanically controlled axe which is between two pieces of wood and when the head is laid upon the block, the rope is let go, and the axe comes down and separates the head from the body, the one falling on one side, the other on the other side'.

However, the machine introduced by Dr Guillotin in 1792 bears greater resemblance to that used in Halifax, Yorkshire from 1286 to 1650, of which an excellent description has come down to us in Holinshed's *Chronicles* of 1587.

There is, and has been, of ancient time, a law or rather a custom at Halifax that whosoever doth commit a felony and is caught either hand habend or back berand, that is, having the stolen goods either in his hand or bearing them on his back, or confesses the fact upon examination, if it be valued by four constables to amount to the sum of thirteen-halfpenny, he is forthwith upon one of the next market days or on the same day if it is a market day, to be beheaded.

The engine wherewith the execution is done is a square block of wood, of the length of four and a half feet, which doth ride up and down in a slot between two pieces of timber that are framed and set upright, of five yards in height. In the lower end of the sliding block is a blade keyed or fastened into the wood which, being drawn up into the frame, is there fastened by a wooden pin.

Into the middle of the pin is a long rope fastened, that cometh down among the people, so that when the offender has made his confession and hath laid his neck over the base block, every man there doth either take hold of the rope, or putteth forth his arm as near to the rope as he can, in token that he is willing to see justice done. Pulling out the pin in this manner, the block wherein the blade is fastened doth fall down with such a violence that even if the neck of the transgressor be as thick as a bull, it would still be cut asunder at a stroke, and roll from the body by a huge distance.

If it is so that the offender be apprehended for stealing an ox, sheep, kine or any such animal, that same beast or another of its kind shall have the end of the rope tied to it and on being driven away shall draw out the pin, whereby the offender shall be executed.

That the head certainly did roll far from the body is evidenced by the Halifax historian Wright in his account of a woman who rode along Gibbet Street, where the beheading machine stood on its stone base on Gibbet Hill. As the block thundered down, its force propelled the severed head into the basket she carried in front of her on the saddle. Constant recounting of this tale embroidered it further, describing the woman's horror as the head, missing the basket, gripped her apron and held on with its teeth!

The first recorded execution in the town's register is that of Richard Bentley of Sowerby on 20 March 1541. The machine was last used on 30 April 1650 when two men, caught stealing thirty yards of cloth and two horses, were found guilty and as stated in the court records:

> 'Whereas by ancient custom and liberty of Halifax, the said John Wilkinson and Anthony Mitchell are to suffer death by having their heads severed and cut off from their bodies at the Halifax Gibbet. Unto which verdict we subscribe our names.'

After that the structure was dismantled, but a fine replica now stands on the old stone base, with its blade securely immobilized. The original blade, however, has survived and is now on display in the Piece Hall Pre-Industrial Museum. It weighs seven pounds twelve ounces, is ten and a half inches long and nine inches wide.

There is little reason to doubt the efficiency of this

engine of justice. Another advantage was that the release
of the blade was determined not by a State-appointed
employee, but by the action of the anonymous multitude
present in the town's market place. Now that's
democracy!

The canny Scots, never ones to ignore a good invention
when they saw one, thought the Halifax device worthy of
adoption. James Douglas, Earl of Morton, Regent of
Scotland, a politically powerful figure who opposed Mary
Queen of Scots, made occasional visits to London and,
whilst returning from one such trip in 1565, passed
through Halifax. It was probably a market day, with the
added attraction of an execution on Gibbet Hill, and so
impressed was the Earl that he had a model made of the
machine.

Back in Scotland he ordered a full-sized version to be
constructed, and it was known as the Scottish Maiden, the
name perhaps being derived from the Celtic *mod-dun*, the
place where justice was administered.

It was made of oak and consisted of a single horizontal
beam five feet in length on which were mounted two
upright posts ten feet in height, each being four inches
wide, three and a half inches thick, with bevelled corners.
The posts were twelve inches apart and were braced by
lengths of timber attached to the ends of the base beam
and secured to the upright posts four feet from the
ground.

The tops of the posts were fixed into a cross rail two feet
in length, the posts themselves having copper-lined
grooves in their inner faces, in which the axe slid. This
blade consisted of a plate of iron faced with steel,
measuring thirteen inches in length and ten and a half
inches in breadth, sharpened at its edge and weighted at
its upper side with a seventy-pound lead block.

Three and a quarter feet from the bottom a transverse
bar joined the two posts, on which the victim rested his
neck. The bar, eight inches broad and four and a half
inches thick, had a wide groove along its upper surface
filled with lead to resist the impact of the blade. An iron
bar, hinged to one upright, was lowered in order to press

on the victim's neck, making it impossible for him to withdraw his head.

The Maiden was sited near the City Cross in Edinburgh's High Street and, unlike its Halifax counterpart, was operated by the official executioner, the Laird of the Scaffold, rather than the town's citizens. It was in action less than a year after its completion, being blooded, literally, by the execution of some of the murderers of Rizzio, the unpopular secretary of Mary Queen of Scots, on 9 March 1566. It claimed over a hundred victims, one of the more notable being the very man who had brought it from England, the Earl of Morton himself! Falling victim to political intrigue at Court, he was accused of conspiracy in the murder of Darnley, the Scottish Queen's husband.

In 1581 he was led to the Maiden and the executioner pulled the cord, releasing the blade. When the head fell into the waiting basket it was impaled on a pike and exhibited on the nearby Tolbooth for all to see.

Seventy or so years later, in 1650, James Graham, Marquis of Montrose, was found guilty of supporting Charles I and, in the Grassmarket in Edinburgh was hanged, drawn and quartered on a thirty-foot high gallows. His head too was spiked on the Tolbooth. His great enemies, Archibald Campbell, Marquis of Argyll, nicknamed the 'glae-eyed marquis' because of his squint, together with his wife, gloated over Montrose's death, little realizing what Fate's swinging pendulum had in store for them.

In May 1661 Campbell himself, accused of treason, was similarly sentenced to death. Not for him the rope though; the blade of the Maiden descended and his head was taken by the executioner to replace that of his ex-enemy Montrose on the Tolbooth's roof.

The Marchioness had lost her husband, but worse was to follow. Her son, the Earl of Argyll, threw in his lot with the Rye House conspirators, plotting to put James, Duke of Monmouth on the English throne. Captured, he was marched up Canongate and the High Street to the castle from which he had once escaped, and there condemned to death. The rebel Duke had suffered five strokes of the axe;

Argyll, bowing his neck beneath the Maiden's pendent blade, commented wryly that 'it was the sweetest maiden he's ever kissed'.

His head, parboiled, replaced that of his father on the city's gaol, where it remained for many years. The misguided Earl had one claim to fame, being the last man to be executed by the Scottish Maiden, and in 1710 it was dismantled. Its blade and other component parts are now in the National Museum of Antiquities of Scotland, in Edinburgh.

Meanwhile, over in France, they were making do with the sword and the rope, breaking on the wheel and burning at the stake, depending on the crime committed and the social class of the offender.

It was on 10 October 1789 that a certain deputy for Paris, Dr Joseph Ignace Guillotin, proposed to the Constituent Assembly that, among other judicial measures to ensure social equality, the same death penalty should be imposed on all offenders regardless of their rank, and that there should be no penalty more severe than decapitation. Other political issues intervened and it was not until 3 May 1791 that the decree whereby every person condemned to death should be beheaded was passed, although little thought was given to the actual method.

The problems posed were considerable. Under the old French laws the different death-dealing methods coped adequately with the large number of criminals, but if they had all to be executed in the same manner, practical details would make it impossible. Just how could every eligible felon be beheaded by the sword, the only decapitation method currently available?

For expert advice Dr Guillotin turned to Monsieur de Paris, the capital's executioner, Charles-Henri Sanson. So clear was his description of the difficulties involved that his reply is worth quoting in full.

> In order to accomplish the execution in accordance with the intention of the law it is necessary, even without any opposition on the part of the prisoner, that the executioner should be very skilful and the condemned man very

steady, otherwise it would be impossible to accomplish an execution with the sword. After each execution the sword is no longer in a condition to perform another, being likely to break in two; it is absolutely necessary that it should be ground and sharpened afresh if there be several prisoners to execute at the same time. It would be needful therefore to have a sufficient number of swords all ready. This involves very great, indeed almost unsurmountable difficulties.

It must further be pointed out that swords have very often broken in the performance of such executions, and the Paris executioner possesses only two, at a cost of 600 livres each.

It must also be taken into account that, when there are several condemned persons to be executed at the same time, the terror produced by this method of execution, owing to the immense amount of blood that is shed and flows everywhere, creates fear and weakness in the hearts of those who are waiting to die, however intrepid they may be. An attack of faintness forms an invincible obstacle to an execution. If prisoners cannot hold themselves up, and yet the executioner proceeds with the matter, the execution becomes a struggle and a massacre.

Even in the case of other modes of execution, very far from requiring the accuracy demanded by the sword, one has seen prisoners turning faint at the sight of their confederates' death, or at least showing signs of weakness and fear; all this is an argument against execution by beheading with the sword.

In other methods of execution it was very easy to hide these signs of weakness from the public because it was not necessary for their accomplishment that a prisoner should be firm and fearless (e.g. tied to the wheel or at the stake), but with the sword method, if the prisoner moved, the execution failed. How can one control a man who either will not or cannot hold himself still?

Succinctly put; in other words, when it comes to multiple beheadings, swords are non-starters. And the need for a vastly superior method was going to become even more urgent, had they but known it, for in a matter of months the Revolution would be demanding the heads of thousands of hated aristocrats to be removed, somehow or other.

The secretary of the Academy of Surgery, Dr Louis, also expressed an opinion, recommending that:

> some mechanical means be adopted as in England whereby the body of the criminal is laid between two posts, joined by a cross beam at the top, whence the convex hatchet is made to fall on the neck by means of a trigger. The beam of the instrument should be heavy and strong enough to act efficaciously, like the ram used for sinking piles in the ground; we know that its force increases in proportion to the height from which it falls.

So concise was the worthy doctor's description that the eventual beheading device was originally called a Louisette, but that of Deputy Guillotin prevailed. By April 1792 a prototype had not only been constructed, together with a leather bag in which to deposit the head, but had been tested on corpses, commencing with those of women, their slimmer necks proving no obstacle to the falling blade. Sanson, present with his brothers and son, together with sundry medical men and journalists, expressed his satisfaction with the trials, subject to minor modifications.

So how closely did the new machine resemble the Halifax design? Basically it was quite similar, for it consisted of two six-inch thick oak uprights, ten feet high, secured twelve inches apart by a top cross-piece and mounted on a high base. An inch-deep groove, cut vertically down the inner of each upright, provided channels in which ran the blade. This was six inches in depth and weighed fifteen pounds, with an iron block of up to sixty-five pounds mounted on top in order to increase the speed of descent.

The blade was originally crescent-shaped but was replaced by one of a triangular configuration, apparently on the suggestion of the King, Louis XVI. The accuracy of his advice was confirmed when, nine months later, it severed his own head.

The blade was held in the raised position by a rope

which passed through a ring at its top, both ends passing through brass pulleys mounted high on each upright. The two lengths of rope then hung down the outsides of the uprights and were secured there.

A four-inch block of wood, scooped out to take the victim's neck, was bolted to the base of the uprights. This block, eight inches high, had a transverse slit across its top to allow the blade to penetrate its depth, ensuring complete separation of head from body. Attached to the block was an iron crescent which pressed the victim's neck down on the block and so held the head immobile. The apt phrase at the time was 'to look through the little window'!

Where the guillotine improved on the Halifax design was the inbuilt facility to position the victim accurately and quickly in the machine. The Halifax gibbet required the felon to kneel down, an awkward position for one who could be half-fainting with fear and on the point of collapse. The guillotine neatly solved this by having a narrow bench extending from the neck-block at right angles to the uprights, and at its free end was hinged a plank to which the victim was quickly strapped while standing facing the guillotine, the chief executioner securing his left arm, one assistant his right arm and the other assistant his legs. This plank was then pivoted into a horizontal position, slid forward to place the victim's neck between the two uprights, and the iron crescent was dropped into place. Interestingly, the hinged plank was known as the 'bascule', the name also given to the two hinged sections of the roadway of Tower Bridge, adjacent to the English execution site.

Upon the release of the two ropes, the blade would fall, the severed head then dropping into a basket lined with oil-cloth, ghoulishly nicknamed the 'family picnic basket', for subsequent conveyance to the local cemetery.

The actual operation took longer to describe than to enact, for Sanson was to achieve so much expertise when later executing hundreds of aristocrats that he had been known to dispatch twelve victims in thirteen minutes; a mercifully quick end for those condemned to die.

The first live victim of the new machine was Nicholas-Jacques Pelletier who, wearing the obligatory red shirt, was taken to the place de Grève where stood the red-painted guillotine. There, on 25 April 1792, he was decapitated, the machine working perfectly, much to the satisfaction of the authorities, though the watching crowds were disappointed by the speed of the operation and its lack of dramatic spectacle. 'Give us back our wooden gallows!' they chanted.

The newspapers of the day, however, praised the guillotine as being severe without being cruel, quick in action and impersonal. Its immediate success led to other cities demanding one and in the following months eighty guillotines all over France were busy beheading criminals, the municipal executioners doubtless going on a crash course to learn how to operate them.

As word spread about the newfangled invention and more people saw it in action, the guillotine became a public craze. It was nicknamed the 'People's Avenger', the 'Patriotic Shortener', the 'National Razor' and the 'Red Theatre'. Manufacturers made little models of it as toys for children to play with, larger ones as novelties for their parents. The latter replicas came complete with effigies of famous figures of the day which, when beheaded at the dinner table, emitted 'blood', actually expensive liqueur or perfume.

Brooches too bore the image of the guillotine and gold and silver ear-rings in the shape of the device adorned many a trendy mademoiselle. Bawdy songs described the machine's action and its victims' reactions, and stage plays used full-sized versions, carefully rendered inoperable. Criticism of such morbid practices would be unfair. The English too had their similar songs about Anne Boleyn and others, and the author possesses several Victorian brass door-knockers and letter-racks in the form of the executioner with his axe and block!

On 10 August 1792 the storming of the Tuileries Palace heralded the start of the Terror, during which, by decree of the People's Representatives, over 20,000 enemies of the State would be decapitated. All was ready; the machines were proven, their operators trained; now to dispatch their prey.

The executioner of Paris at that time, as mentioned earlier, was Charles-Henri Sanson. He was one of a family who provided the nation with executioners from 1635 to 1889, and this hierarchy of headsmen, this dynasty of decapitators, thrived for more than six generations. Charles-Henri himself was one of seven brothers, all of whom dominated French scaffolds, as did his father, grandfather and great-grandfather. His sisters married executioners, and his sons and grandson followed in his blood-stained footsteps.

Sanson was born in 1739 and grew up in a household ruled by the scaffold. No other career was considered or indeed was possible, and so when his father Jean-Baptiste was stricken with paralysis in 1754 Charles-Henri, being the eldest son, was appointed his deputy despite being only fifteen years old. Within weeks he received his baptism, presiding over his assistants as they executed a murderer, a man sentenced to be broken on the wheel. This involved the felon having his limbs shattered by iron bars, inflicting excruciating agony until death ensued.

This barbaric penalty was ultimately banned in 1788 but Charles-Henri had plenty of other judicial implements at his disposal as he started his career on the scaffold and he quickly assumed the mantle of his calling. He had grown into a tall, strong youth and, in contrast to his English counterparts of the day, was well educated and musically talented, excelling with both violin and violoncello. Mindful of his standing in the city, his clothes were of the finest, setting new styles in 'Sanson Green' among the members of Paris's fashionable society.

His official uniform was very different, however. In the early days he wore the traditional blue breeches and red jacket, the latter being embroidered with the gibbet and a ladder in black. A pink two-cornered hat completed the attire, together with a sword at his waist (for personal defence, not for execution purposes). But by 1786 he was given *carte blanche* in his official dress and so adopted a long double-breasted frock coat of dark green material,

worn with a wide white cravat and striped trousers. A tall
top hat covered his long sandy hair, for while fashionable
white wigs were worn socially, they would have been
ruined by blood splashes whilst on duty.

Later in his career his apparel altered yet again, and he
took to wearing an elegant short jacket and breeches, with
silk stockings and bright buckled shoes. A tricorne hat
completed his appearance with, of course, the customary
sword.

French executioners, of which there were many, identified themselves by the towns they served, and Charles-
Henri thus became Monsieur de Paris, though he added
other more imposing titles, 'Exécuteur des Jugements
Criminels' and 'Executioner of the High Works'. 'Admiral
of the Red' was another, because he strode the bloody
boards. Even more impressive was 'Chevalier de Longval',
a title reflecting the family's belief in its noble ancestry.
Charles-Henri even sported a coat of arms which, featuring
a cracked bell, was a pun on *sans son*, without sound. And
his nickname 'Charlot' was given to later French executioners, just as 'Jack Ketch' became the accepted name for
all English hangmen.

The executioner's duties were many and varied.
Together with his leather-aproned assistants, he carried
out the court's orders, securing felons in the pillory,
whipping and branding others. The pillory, sited on top of a
tower adjoining Sanson's house, could be rotated to expose
its occupant to the maximum of public abuse. Whipping
was administered using a bundle of long flexible birch
twigs, whilst branding marked the victim for life with
letters signifying his or her crime.

But it was when public executions took place that
Charles-Henri's skills brought the crowds to watch and
applaud. Prior to the introduction of the guillotine in 1792,
the rope and sword were the major instruments of death.
As at Tyburn, hanging was accomplished by making the
felon mount a ladder, the noose about his neck. Once at the
top, he would be 'turned off', the ladder being twisted away
to leave him suspended from the beam. And so it was the
ladder which symbolically decorated the executioner's

tunic as a sinister badge of his trade.

So when the Terror came Sanson, having helped to perfect the guillotine, was ready and equipped with the ultimate means of execution. The tumbrils rumbled over the cobbles, delivering their cargoes of men and women innocent of all crime except that of being an aristocrat, an enemy of the Republic. They were tied to the wooden sides of the carts, their hands bound behind them, their feet bare, their hair cut short by the executioner before leaving the prison.

Sanson, far from considering himself the instrument of vengeance, was sickened by the sheer enormity of his task as he and his team worked almost mechanically, literally decapitating the condemned as fast as they mounted the scaffold. As many as forty, sometimes fifty, would arrive in a fleet of tumbrils, to be herded into line and beheaded, one every two minutes.

Blood constantly soaked the scaffold, making it almost too slippery for the executioners to stand up. It dripped down between the boards, so that metal netting had to be fixed round the sides to keep the dogs away. Blood ran into the gutters, mixing with the mud in the street so that the footsteps of passers-by were evident by the crimson trail they left on the cobbles.

As a partial solution a hole was dug beneath the scaffold and filled with sand which was frequently renewed, but the smell of decomposing blood was so appalling that the authorities considered using a lead-lined container on a small trolley to convey the blood away at the end of each day.

As the batches of bodies reached the cemeteries, officials stripped them of their clothes and the corpses were then dumped into deep trenches. Bonfires blazed nearby, casting a Dante-like glow over the funereal proceedings as other men sorted the blood-stiffened clothing into various piles, there to be recorded by a clerk. After being washed in the river the clothes were then distributed to charitable institutions.

At the height of the Terror, Sanson and his assistants guillotined 300 men and women in three days, 1,300 in six weeks, and between 6 April 1793 and 29 July 1795, no fewer than 2,831 heads dropped into the baskets.

As required by the State, Sanson had to continue the legal slaughter, knowing that his refusal would simply have led to his own death and his instant replacement by another executioner. Never a callous man, he tried to alleviate the suffering of the doomed whenever possible rather than yield to the crowd's demand for more brutality.

His victims came from all walks of life, bishops, generals, lawyers and artists, together with the high-born of both sexes. Of all the aristocratic victims, perhaps the executions of three women were the most tragic. Not all were 'society butterflies'; indeed one, Marie-Anne Charlotte Corday d'Armont, better known by her middle names, was a zealous supporter of the Revolution but recoiled from the bloodthirsty measures demanded by leader Marat who called for the deaths of nearly half a million of the upper classes.

Accordingly, she left home in Normandy and, entering Marat's Paris house, found him in his bathtub. Without hesitating she stabbed him to death with an ebony-handled knife, then waited patiently to be arrested. 'I have killed a villain to save innocent people,' she exclaimed.

After her trial Sanson came to the prison to prepare her for execution, to find that her picture was being painted by an artist for the official records. While she posed, wearing a red skirt – obligatory for her dreaded destination – Sanson sheared her long hair, and Charlotte gave a strand of it to the artist, as a souvenir.

When Sanson began to tie her hands behind her, she asked whether she was allowed to wear her gloves, so that the straps would not chafe her wrists, and the executioner, impressed by her calm mien, desisted and left her hands free. Vast crowds lined the route, and from a balcony three other leaders of the Revolution watched the 'assassin's' procession. Little did they realize that they too, Desmoulins, Danton and Robespierre, would also accompany Sanson to the guillotine in the not too distant future.

On the scaffold Charlotte approached the bascule. 'Is

this what I have to do?' she asked. Instantly Sanson and his assistant positioned her, sliding the plank forward, and the executioner released the blade before she realized what was happening. A duty carpenter, Le Gros, exceeding his office, then seized the girl's severed head and, holding it up high, slapped one cheek in exultation, his action so infuriating Sanson that he had Le Gros immediately dismissed from his job, though the man was later reinstated under pressure from the authorities.

The Queen, Marie Antoinette, was of course a prime target for the mob, being accused of treason against the people and even of committing obscenities with her eight-year-old son. Incarcerated for over three months, guarded day and night by soldiers, allowed no privacy whatsoever, her hair had turned grey and she grew pale and emaciated. The Revolutionary court sentenced her to death and on 16 October 1793 the crowds gathered behind the soldiers lining the streets and the drums beat their staccato dirge.

A gaoler's wife brought the royal prisoner a cup of chocolate and a bread roll, and screened the Queen from the soldiers as she dressed in a white gown, with a muslin shawl about her shoulders, and a small white cap on her head. Sanson arrived, to bind her hands behind her with rope and to cut off her hair.

The tumbril awaited, pulled by a white horse, and to the accompaniment of continual abuse and jeers from the mob, she mounted the cart and the procession set off for the Tuileries Gardens. There, helped by Sanson, Marie-Antoinette climbed the scaffold steps, reportedly losing a shoe 'of black silk, shabby and full of holes' as she did so, a valuable memento indeed for the finder.

Sanson wrote later that on the scaffold she accidentally stepped on his foot, and hastily apologized, but before she finished the words she had been pressed against the waiting bascule. Then followed the three most dreaded sounds to be heard in France: the loud bang as the plank swung horizontally to strike its bench, the metallic clang as the lunette, the iron collar, was swung across to pin the victim's neck down, followed almost immediately by the reverberating crash as the weighted blade fell, severing her head and jarring against the block beneath, the impact shaking the whole structure.

Next moment the head was lifted from the basket and shown to the jeering mob, before her remains were placed in a box and removed to be burnt in quicklime.

Charlotte Corday, the Queen and nearly all the other victims of the guillotine maintained a proud dignity right to the end, denying the mob the satisfaction of witnessing their fear or humiliation. One exception however was Jeanne Becu Gomard de Vaubernier, Comtesse du Barry, mistress of the late Louis XV and, ironically enough, an old acquaintance of Charles-Henri Sanson.

Jeanne du Barry, the niece of an old friend of the Sanson family, was a girl who, despite her early convent training, had a liking for the boys, a partiality which led to her dismissal from the convent. She took a job in Paris, in the rue St Honoré, where her attractions soon brought her a host of admirers. Charles-Henri was one who found her charming, but twenty-seven years were to elapse before they met again, and then it was his duty to behead her.

Madam du Barry had actually escaped to England when the Terror broke out, but had misguidedly returned, thinking that because she was one of the people and not born an aristocrat, she would be safe in her own country. But the Revolution allowed of no excuses; a king's mistress was as doomed as a duchess. And despite her frantic pleas, her offers of bribes, of hidden jewellery, she was sentenced to death.

On collecting her from the Hall of the Dead, Sanson was shocked by her ravaged, bloated appearance, her desperate efforts to evade him as he attempted to tie her hands and cut her hair. So wild were her screams in the tumbril that the crowds fell silent, seemingly too ashamed to jeer at such a display of hysteria.

On seeing the scaffold du Barry lost all control. In a frenzy she fought the three men who carried her up the steps, writhing so frantically that it took all of three minutes to strap her to the bascule. Once there Sanson, her erstwhile admirer and friend, stepped forward and dispatched the former Court favourite to the grave.

But the peak of the executioner's career occurred at 10.22 a.m. on 21 January 1793, the moment when the guillotine blade severed the head of King Louis XVI. Earlier that morning His Majesty, with his confessor abbé Edgeworth de Firmont, were led from their prison, the Great Tower of the Temple fortress, to a waiting closed carriage. The doomed monarch, a thickset man of florid complexion, clean shaven, with rather large eyes and a high forehead, wore a white waistcoat beneath his coat, and his breeches and stockings were of grey silk. His companion, the Irishman Edgeworth, although a priest, was forbidden to wear his pastoral habiliment, under a new revolutionary regulation.

The two men climbed in to the large carriage, accompanied by a lieutenant and a sergeant major, both armed with muskets. These weapons were probably to repel any rescue attempt *en route* rather than to shoot their royal prisoner should he try to escape, muskets hardly being practical weapons to use in the close confines of a carriage.

The vehicle was preceded by a contingent of drummers, with armed soldiers riding on each side. The streets were lined by armed citizens and troops as the carriage was driven the two miles to the place de la Révolution, a square packed with more soldiers and citizens of the Republic, its outer perimeter being further guarded by cannon.

At the scaffold Sanson and his two assistants had been waiting for some time, all three armed with daggers and pistols, Sanson's concealed beneath his long green double-breasted coat, his deputies hiding their weapons under their leather aprons. A last-minute endeavour by royalists to save the King at all costs could not be ruled out.

When the King arrived, he removed his coat, unfastened his collar and opened his shirt. As Sanson stepped forward to tie his hands, Louis indignantly protested but then permitted the executioner to do his duty. Climbing the steep steps with the assistance of the abbé, the King made a short speech, the words being drowned by the incessant tattoo of the two-score drummers surrounding the scaffold.

There was little Sanson could do to ease the King's plight other than expedite the procedure. Accordingly he and his assistants quickly secured their royal victim to the bascule, and then Charles-Henri released the blade.

As the crash of its impact echoed around the square scores of spectators joined hands in a circle, dancing joyfully and singing the Marseillaise. Others shouted 'Now the tyrant's head lies low!' But Sanson wasted no time. Even as one assistant held the head high on display, Charles-Henri placed the body in a long wicker basket, then took the head, its face pale, the eyes wide open, and laid it on the corpse's legs.

On the executioner's cart, the basket was transported to the Church of the Madeleine where, after a short religious ceremony, the remains, now in a pinewood coffin, were buried in a grave six feet wide, twelve feet deep, in the cemetery, having first been covered with quicklime.

When the cart returned to the place de la Révolution the wicker basket fell to the ground and was immediately surrounded by the mob who soaked handkerchiefs and pieces of cloth in the King's blood, one man even rubbing a pair of dice over the bloodstained wickerwork.

Far from rejoicing, Sanson felt nothing but remorse at having to kill his king, reportedly kneeling each night before the blade he had used, and praying for the soul of Louis XVI.

By this time Sanson had been the Paris executioner for nearly forty years. His home life, such as it was, was shared with his devoted wife Marie-Anne, whom he had married in 1765. She had borne him two sons who, true to the family tradition, became executioners. Henri, born in 1767, was actively employed during the Terror, learning his trade by constantly helping his father on the scaffold, as did their younger son Gabriel. He, however, came to a macabre, if ironically appropriate end in 1792, by falling off the scaffold whilst holding up the severed head of a forger, doubtless losing his footing on the blood-slippery boards. His death, tragically witnessed by his father, led to railings being erected around the sides of all French scaffolds.

The Sanson family was never really affluent and moreover had many relatives for whom to provide. The executioner's salary barely covered his expenses, insufficient allowances being paid by the authorities for the many extras needed. Sanson had to employ assistants and carters, a blacksmith, a cook and servants. He had to buy the equipment and materials with which to carry out the sentences of the court, the wicker baskets, hatchets, branding irons plus the pomade and gunpowder with which to apply to the burn marks, fetters and ropes, aprons and trousers for his men. Bran, sand and sawdust were necessary to prevent slipping on the boards, as well as straps for the victims and gratuities for the grave-diggers. All this plus the cost of tumbrils, horses, their harnesses and feed, entailed a considerable outlay, and Sanson frequently had to apply for a pay rise.

As in England, though, the job had its perquisites. In the early days of his career Sanson was entitled to claim any valuables in possession of his victims, their clothing and jewellery, and some of these were passed on to his assistants, until a later decree stated that clothing must go to the poor instead. Nevertheless there was always something with which to augment his pay, and when the opportunity arose Sanson sold cadavers to surgeons for medical research. His own knowledge of dissection also paid dividends, allowing him to concoct remedies against rheumatism made from the fat of his hanged victims. Another of his official tasks, as mentioned earlier, was to cut off the hair of those condemned to the guillotine and there was much demand for the flowing locks, which were then made into wigs and worn as grisly trophies.

Another lucrative source of income came Charles-Henri's way when he made the acquaintance of a Swiss, John Christopher Curtius, whose business involved the modelling in wax of human limbs and organs for medical schools. Having extended the business by modelling faces of the famous, capturing likenesses much as today's fashionable photographers, Curtius opened a gallery in Paris and there displayed tableaux of royal groups and also more sinister representations; those of torture and execution. For details of the latter he logically contacted Sanson and so a firm friendship was soon established.

Curtius and his niece, Marie Grosholtz, a gifted sculptress in her own right, quickly grasped the opportunity to model the ill-fated aristocrats, their severed heads being 'loaned' by Sanson *en route* from the scaffold to the cemetery, for copying purposes. So remarkable was Marie's talent that both she and Charles-Henri benefited financially from the arrangement, and the gallery became more famous with every head that fell into Sanson's basket.

At Curtius's death Marie inherited both his gallery and estate, and she continued to reproduce the eerily life-like effigies. In 1795 she married François Tussaud and seven years later moved to England, bringing her exhibition with her, thereby founding Madame Tussaud's Waxworks, a respected institution, which had grown from such bizarre and gory origins.

Whatever profits Sanson made, he was still a public servant, and the Revolution demanded more and more victims. Not only the rich and noble but, as rivalry and bitter infighting grew among the ruling Council, the very founders of the Revolution were delivered into Sanson's care, to suffer as those they had condemned suffered, and the dreaded blade fell on Robespierre, Danton, Fouquier-Tinville, Henriot, even Lebas. This last revolutionary had cheated the State by committing suicide while awaiting execution, but was not allowed to cheat the guillotine. Accompanied by his living colleagues, the corpse was lifted on to the scaffold, placed on the plank and Charles-Henri released the blade, severing the already dead head. Justice had been done!

By 1795 Sanson's arduous way of life started to take its toll. For forty-one years he had used the sword and branding-iron, pillory and guillotine, on countless victims, decapitating nearly 3,000 men and women during the Terror itself. Exhausted and sickened by the bloodshed, he developed nephritis, a kidney complaint which compelled him to submit his resignation on 30 August 1795 and to request a pension. The latter was not granted, the authorities deciding that as he had not been officially appointed public executioner until 1778, less than the stipulated thirty years, he was not eligible to qualify.

Charles-Henri and his wife retired to their house in the country where Sanson relaxed in his garden, planting and pruning. Like an old war horse however, he could not forget the scaffold and on 5 May 1802 he returned to his old profession, guillotining a murderess. This was no cold-blooded obsession with the past though, for on the following day he wrote to the authorities, describing the brutal reactions of the crowd even when a woman was executed, and urging that the death penalty should be imposed only on men.

This was to be his last execution, and the Sansons settled down in Paris. His condition steadily deteriorated and he contented himself with gentle walks near his home. On one such outing in 1806, as recorded among the family documents, Sanson encountered a group of men escorting none other than Napoleon Bonaparte, Consul of France. Being recognized by one of the party, Charles-Henri admitted his identity to Bonaparte. The great man, aware of Sanson's role during the Revolution, asked whether, if circumstances required it, the executioner would guillotine *him*. Charles-Henri replied 'Sire, I executed Louis XVI!' Reportedly Napoleon turned pale at the riposte, then curtly ordered Sanson to leave them.

Shortly after this encounter, Sanson's medical condition worsened and he was forced to take to his bed in the house at No. 10 rue Neuve Saint-Jean. On 4 July 1806 he passed away, the local priests and choir being present at his bedside for his spiritual comfort.

He was buried two days later in grave no. 27 in the Montmartre cemetery after an impressive funeral service in Saint-Laurent Church, the plot being marked by a plain stone in order to avoid possible desecration. It was later engraved with his name, the dates of his birth and death, and the inscription 'This stone was erected by his son and family by whom he was regretted' and although the medical reasons for his death are known, it is said that he, like Richard Brandon, executioner of Charles I, died of sorrow at having to kill his King.

Charles-Henri's wife, Marie-Anne, lived on in Paris with her many relatives until her death on 24 October 1817 at the age of eighty-four. A loyal and caring wife, she had sustained her husband through experiences undreamed of by ordinary men, episodes which by their sheer horror would have daunted even other executioners.

And of course other executioners there were, more than 160 of them, every town of importance having its own Lord of the Scaffold, at least until 1789. The Sanson family dispatched the criminals of Paris, Rheims and Tours, the Fereys taking similar care of felons in Orléans, Rouen and Provins. The Jouennes administered final judgement in Melun, Caen and Dieppe while the Desmoret family reduced the crime wave of Châlons, Epernay and Étampes. Dedicated professionals all, men married other executioners' daughters, their sons became executioners, and their assistants on the scaffold usually had a dual role as their house servants.

Drink was always a problem for some executioners, though it doubtless provided a blessed relief from their horrific duties. Even one of Sanson's brothers, the executioner of Herault, yielded to the temptation, frequently being so drunk that executions had to be postponed.

Another of the great Charles-Henri's relatives, his grandson Henri-Clement, had similar problems. He was the last of the line in the dynasty of Sansons but he was never really suited to his profession. This was never more evident than when, in 1836, would-be assassins attempted to kill King Louis-Philippe by means of a multi-barrelled rifle device. They missed their target but killed eighteen bystanders and injured many more. All the conspirators were sentenced to death, one of them suffering unimaginable horrors when the descending blade jammed, inches above his neck! Desperately Henri-Clement and his assistants freed it, only for it to jam twice again before finally delivering the death stroke.

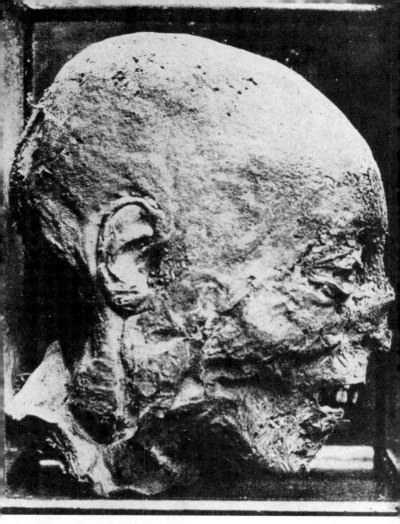

The head of Henry Grey, Duke of Suffolk, father of Lady Jane Grey. He was found guilty of high treason and decapitated by two blows of the axe on Tower Hill, London, on 20 February 1554

Noose with which wife murderer Richard Pedder was hanged at Lancaster Castle in 1857 by executioner William Calcraft, exponent of the 'short drop' method which caused death by strangulation

The electric chair, also known as 'Old Smokey' or the 'Hot Squat', became an increasingly popular form of execution in the United States following its adoption in the State of New York by Governor David B. Hill on 4 June 1888

Margaret, Countess of Salisbury, after having been sentenced without trial and harshly imprisoned in the Tower of London for two years, was brutally beheaded on Tower Green on 27 May 1541

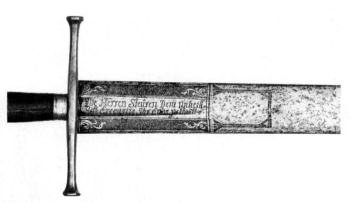

'The judges check evil. I carry out their capital judgement'

A finely balanced, precision instrument of death: a German executioner's sword of about 1700

The 'Halifax Gibbet' was in use in that town from at least 1541 until April 1650. It was probably the only execution device not operated by an official executioner

'Improved' gallows outside Newgate Prison eliminated the grim processions to Tyburn but failed to reduce the suffering endured by the ten felons hanged on 7 December 1783

To be broken on the wheel was a horrific and prolonged execution, the victim's limbs being slowly and systematically shattered with an iron bar, a final blow to the chest bringing merciful death

Tyburn executions in Elizabeth I's reign, as portrayed here, involved hanging, disembowelling and quartering. The heads were then parboiled in a cauldron and spiked on the city's gates

29

The version of the wheel on which Saint Catherine suffered her
martyrdom. This event is commemorated by the modern firework of
the same name

The guillotine was similar to, though much later than the Halifax gibbet and was used in France from 1792. It proved to be an almost instantaneous, virtually painless, but extremely messy method of execution

The Tower's Yeoman Gaoler with the ceremonial axe. It was originally used by him when escorting a prisoner, to indicate to the waiting crowds the verdict of the court; the edge pointing towards the prisoner signifying execution

During the Mexican revolution of the 1860's, rope was evidently in short supply. Hangings were then carried out using telegraph wire – with dire decapitating results

In 1866 Mexicans led by Juarez rebelled against Emperor Maximilian and his supporters. Summary executions by firing squads were frequent and the victims were even denied the benefit of a blindfold

Just as at Tyburn mishaps, the watching crowd turned violent as the executions continued, the executioners having to be rescued by the police. Beneath the strain of a career not of his choosing, Henri-Clement's inclinations later turned elsewhere. As a distraction he started gambling and drinking, spending so much on luxuries that he got into serious debt. To the shame of his family he was sent to the debtors' prison in Paris, despite his claim that he was indispensable to society.

Having frittered away the family's wealth and sold his valuable paintings and antiques, he had only one thing left to pledge to his creditors for his freedom – the guillotine itself! So he pawned it to those he owed money, and during the ensuing weeks doubtless lived in fear and trembling of an impending execution.

Sure enough, in March 1847 he was directed to have the guillotine ready for action. Frantically he pleaded with his debtors to release the machine, if only for the one day, but to no avail. So the guillotine-less executioner had to report the dismal details to the public prosecutor, an interview which regrettably has not been recorded for posterity.

The authorities perforce had to produce the four thousand or so francs required to redeem the machine, but it heralded the finale of Henri-Clement's career as a Lord of the Scaffold.

Joseph Heinderich was appointed in his stead, and on his death in 1872 Nicolas Roch became Monsieur de Paris. By that time not only had the number of offences carrying the death penalty declined in number but the guillotine itself had become somewhat more unobtrusive. No longer a terrifying scarlet on a high scaffold, it had reverted to its natural wood colour and stood at ground level, a new position definitely not welcomed by the crowds.

Fewer victims meant fewer death sentences and so executioners in the provinces retired and, utilizing their professionally acquired anatomical skills, became surgeons' assistants or animal doctors. Others concealed their former trade and sought jobs in a different part of the country, their families at last free to marry outside the 'closed shop' of executioners.

But murderers still had to be beheaded, one sensational case being that of Hélène Jegado, a peasant woman who was guillotined in 1851. Whilst she was employed as a maid in various establishments, other staff members met mysterious deaths, usually from poison. Although charged with only three murders, she was strongly suspected of being the cause of twenty other similar deaths, and was duly beheaded.

Eleven years later, vast crowds again packed round the scaffold for yet another mass murderer, Martin Dumollard, a case also involving house staff. Prospective maids, invited to a lonely house for interview, were never seen alive again, until one escaped and reported her suspicions. A search of the house revealed three corpses and the belongings of many others, and to save her own skin, Mme Dumollard confessed that her husband had murdered the girls for their valuables and clothes. As an accomplice she was sent to the gallows and her husband 'looked through the little window'.

The era of the French Lords of the Scaffold finally came to an end by a decree passed in 1870 which stipulated that all executions in France were to be carried out by Monsieur de Paris, Nicolas Roch, he being succeeded in 1879 by Louis Deibler. Provincial guillotines and scaffolds were dismantled and those not exhibited in museums were broken up and scrapped. No more would their bascules swing down, their blades thunder along the grooves, their baskets rock as they received the severed heads.

Yet it was that very aspect which fascinated the medical profession, whose members still conjectured whether, because of the speed of the decapitation, the brain could continue to function, albeit for only a matter of seconds. After all, they reasoned, execution by the guillotine or sword differed markedly from that dealt by the axe. The latter crushed its way through the vertebrae and tissues, probably rendering the victim unconscious through the shock of its initial impact. The razor-sharp edge of the sword or guillotine however, struck the victim cleanly, slicing its way through so swiftly that the victim was probably unaware of it happening, in much the same way as, when using a sharp kitchen knife, it is not apparent that one has cut one's hand until the blood actually appears.

It could be argued therefore that the life force continued to flow through the brain for an unknown length of time after such a decapitation; that perhaps a victim *could* see the basket coming up to meet him or her, *did* hear the triumphant shouts of the mob. Perhaps Anne Boleyn's lips moved in real protest when her head was held high on Tower Green, and was mute only because of her severed vocal chords. Maybe Charlotte Corday really did blush with humiliation when Le Gros smacked her cheek after she had been guillotined.

French doctors carried out various macabre experiments to verify such hypotheses. Some, as reported in the newspapers of the day, pumped blood through a severed head, then watched engrossed as the lips twitched and the eyelids flickered. Others attended an execution and, immediately following the decapitation, called the victim by name, whereupon the eyes opened and focused for up to half a minute before glazing over. But no conclusions were reached as to whether the movements were deliberate or just reflex contractions of the muscles after death, and the problem seems unlikely ever to be resolved.

Although the number of executions dwindled during the nineteenth century, the guillotine once again became as popular a public attraction as in earlier days. It mattered not that the victims were now criminals rather than aristocrats. The spectators gathered in their thousands, surging with excitement, the tension rising as the hour approached, the ghoulish anticipation rippling through the crowd as the executioner and his assistant prepared the device which, even though on the ground, towered over the assembly like an altar of death.

As big an attraction as London's Lord Mayor's Show or the State Opening of Parliament, so in Paris the crowds flocked to see the 'National Razor' at work. Nor was it of only local interest, for in 1889 Thomas Cook's travel agency advertised the executions of Allorto and Sellier as a tourist attraction and filled nearly 300 seats in the fleet of horse-buses they had chartered. A Victorian equivalent of a package tour, it probably included a visit to the Moulin Rouge and an ascent of the Eiffel Tower as well.

The tourists would hardly have been impressed by the then master of ceremonies Louis Deibler who, despite his long service both as assistant and chief executioner, was frequently castigated by the French press for his hesitant and maladroit conduct, the ineptness of his performances contributing little to the merciful dispatch of his victims.

In 1899 Louis was succeeded by his son Anatole who, although bearded and muscular like his father, was incomparably more efficient. A true professional, he beheaded his victims with unhurried expertise, a credit to his calling.

Following the turn of the century and the appalling death toll in France during the First World War, it might have been thought that the public's appetite for human blood sports had been satiated, but the pulling power of the awesome machine, the reverberating crash of the descending blade, was just as strong as ever. Most executions drew vast crowds, none more so than the execution of 52-year-old Henri Landru in 1922. The case attracted newspaper reporters from all over the world, for despite his unprepossessing appearance he had an animal magnetism that women found irresistible.

During his trial in a packed courtroom, it was stated that he had had only to advertise in newspapers for a companion, and affluent widows queued up at the postboxes, no fewer than 300 of them having been eager to meet their 'Monsieur Right'. Those who were invited to his house in the country contributed involuntarily to the thick pall of black smoke which occasionally poured from the chimney, an effusion which, however, caused little comment in those non-environment-friendly days. But a friend of a missing widow grew suspicious, and when the police found Landru's gruesome diary and the charred remains of women in his stove, the game was up.

On 25 February 1922 Anatole Deibler prepared Landru

by clipping the hair at the nape of his neck and cutting a wide half-moon of material from his shirt and collar. The executioner and his two bowler-hatted assistants then escorted the portly, balding murderer to the scaffold, where the mounted gendarmes raised their swords in salute.

While the multitude of spectators watched, Deibler secured the condemned man and, without a second's hesitation, the blade was released, the red-bearded head falling into the waiting basket.

Anatole Deibler continued to grace the scaffold during those postwar years, earning the public's unstinted praise until, after dispatching more than 300 victims, he died in 1939.

In that year the renowned Henri Desfourneaux assumed command of the scaffold. He played a major part in the executions of Second World War criminals and others, nearly 1,500 men and women being guillotined during the twelve years of his reign as Monsieur de Paris.

In addition to his outstanding public service, Henri made his mark in his profession's history by being the last French executioner to perform in public. For although executions before English crowds ended in 1868, it was not until 1939 that France decided to follow suit and withdraw the scaffold behind prison walls.

The last occasion on which the ghastly spectacle was enacted in public occurred on 18 June 1939, the scene in front of the Palais de Justice in Versailles being little different from those during the Terror. The condemned man was Eugen Weidmann, a merciless killer who had committed six murders, shooting and robbing four men and two women.

His execution had been timed for 5 a.m., in the hope that it would be too early for the crowds to gather, but such a subterfuge did not deter the guillotine devotees. They packed the square throughout the night, filling every balcony and window overlooking the scaffold, drinking and singing to while away the time. And when morning came, so wild was the applause which greeted Henri Desfourneaux, so vile the abuse hurled at the victim

Weidmann, that the whole sorry episode brought about its own solution. One week later a decree was passed confining all executions to the privacy of the prison yard, where sentences could be carried out in a more humane and dignified manner.

In 1951 Desfourneaux was succeeded by André Obrecht who dispatched over thirty criminals during his term of office. But eventually the guillotine became little used, only eight executions taking place between 1965 to 1977.

By the 1970s a much improved guillotine had become available for the few who required it. Its working parts were manufactured of materials less likely to jam, and other minor modifications were incorporated to reduce even further the time needed to dispatch the victim. Spirit levels ensured that the device was on an even keel so that the blade fell true, and the inevitable drenching of the assistant by the blood which spurted from the corpse's neck was eliminated by the fitting of a transparent shield. A hygienic bucket replaced the traditional wicker basket as a receptacle for the head, and a zinc-lined container subsequently received the body.

Despite these modern innovations however, the French judicial system changed in order to reflect public opinion, ultimately deciding that executions should no longer have a place in society. The last guillotine execution was in 1977. And by a decree of September 1981, capital punishment was abolished.

This chapter should not close without mentioning a controversy which arose among historians and researchers earlier this century, as to the real identity of the originator of the French guillotine. While most authorities credit Dr Joseph Ignace Guillotin with its conception, some historians believed that it was more the brainchild of the good doctor's cousin, a man who was also a doctor, also called Joseph Guillotin, but lacked the name 'Ignace'.

Perhaps because of this similarity of names and profession, confusion could have arisen in the old archival records, some of which suggested that cousin Joseph played the more active role in the innovation of the beheading machine, while Joseph Ignace, being a deputy of the Assembly, was better placed to bring the idea to the notice of the government of the day.

Certainly cousin Joseph's background lends credence to this possibility, for he studied medicine, qualifying as a doctor in 1775 and setting up a practice in Nantes before moving to Paris to become the prison doctor at the Châtelet prison. He furthered his interest in judicial punishment by visiting English and Scottish gaols, where he would have had every opportunity to learn about the Halifax gibbet and Scottish Maiden.

Back in his home country he met and fell in love with Eugénie de Launey, daughter of the King's Lieutenant General at Nantes, having rescued her from a gang of highwaymen. Unfortunately her father, having other plans for her future betrothal, suspected Joseph of falsifying the attack and sent his men to capture the eloping couple in their flight to safety in England.

Ambushed, Eugénie was caught but Joseph got away to London. And on hearing that her father had forced her into an arranged marriage with the Marquise de Kersaint, Joseph became a fanatical anti-royalist, involving himself in the radical conspiracies of the day.

When social upheaval in France appeared inevitable, he returned to Paris and, according to one theory, perfected the guillotine with the assistance of his cousin Joseph Ignace. Involved deeply in the Revolution, he discovered that not only Eugénie, but her husband and daughter were held in prison awaiting execution and, despite all his efforts, all three were beheaded on the scaffold.

Devastated, he deserted the revolutionary regime and secretly supported the royalist faction by plotting the downfall of Robespierre and the other leaders. Even when Napoleon came to power, Joseph Guillotin continued his efforts on behalf of the monarchists.

But the republican counter-espionage was highly organized, and early in 1814 he was arrested, tried and condemned to death. And on 26 March 1814, only weeks before his cousin Ignace died of pneumonia, Joseph mounted the steps where Henri Sanson, son of the renowned Charles-Henri, greeted him by saying, 'Now you will know if the

''Widow's Kiss'' is indeed pleasant.'

Joseph Guillotin replied: 'I will place myself in the right position and it will not hurt. But first take this diary, which contains the story of my life.'

He lay on the plank which pivoted him forward and Sanson released the blade; the very one, the story goes, which had severed the head of his beloved Eugénie.

The diary, torn and bloodstained, was later discovered in the official archives, bearing on its last page a comment by Henri Sanson: 'Poor devil, I did him a service when I released the blade.'

So who really devised the guillotine – Doctor Joseph Ignace Guillotin, Deputy of the Assembly? Or Doctor Joseph Guillotin, prison doctor, thwarted lover and vengeful plotter? Many people still believe that, just as the Earl of Morton fell prey to the Scottish Maiden, the machine which he had introduced, so Doctor Guillotin died beneath the blade of his brainchild, the National Razor. But which Doctor Guillotin? And would it not be poetic justice if he who had devised it, eventually died by it?

4   Rulers of the Rope

They executed wrongdoers, they provided society with a popular entertainment, and their art enriched the English language with a new and picturesque vocabulary. When they performed, tradesmen prospered by supplying spectators with refreshments, pickpockets dipped deep and often into strangers' pockets, owners of 'ringside' balconies and windows waxed fat. Innkeepers on the scaffold route boosted their sales and medical students ultimately increased their anatomical knowledge. It was, for hundreds of years, a growth industry, based on the attraction of seeing some poor wretch or wretches dying from slow strangulation.

For centuries, disposing of criminals by hanging them was the standard method in England and indeed in many other countries, for lengths of rope were cheap and although the gallows had to be built high, those were the only overheads. In the early days all that was needed was a hurdle, a rope over a beam and a ladder; and, of course, that dominating personality, the Lord of the Scaffold, with an assistant. After being dragged on a hurdle from prison to execution site, the victim climbed the ladder for the noose to be secured, and then the ladder was twisted, 'turning off' the felon and leaving his feet kicking in the empty air.

The public loved it. Muskets were too quick and noisy, the axe also too quick, and messy. Guillotines were too mechanical, all right for fancy foreigners, but for sheer spectacle and prolonged drama, one couldn't beat a good old English hanging.

An old Victorian guidebook included a reportedly

factual account of spectators' conversations at a hanging in the early nineteenth century, and could well be typical of those at any execution:

> The clock strikes 8 a.m. and an official bids all present to be silent. The fateful doors swing open and
>
> 'Oh Lord, oh Lord!' exclaims a woman. 'There's the parson!'
>
> 'One – two – three – there's Jack – God bless him!'
>
> 'How lovely he looks – dressed as if for a wedding!' sobs another woman. 'And there's Tom – he sees me – he sees me – God be with you, Tom!'
>
> 'And God bless them all!' cries another female, bursting into tears.
>
> 'Why, there's only four of them!' exclaims a spectator with a whining tone of disappointment.
>
> 'There must be six,' says another. 'Six was the number, but there's only strings [nooses] for four, so two must have been reprieved.'
>
> 'Parson's shaking their hands – the Lord bless them!'
>
> 'How Tom stands, like a rock! What pluck! Doesn't shake a finger! Keep up, Tom!'
>
> 'Hangman's gone below!' cries a woman, her voice suddenly husky, fixing her nails like a beast of prey in the arm of her companion. 'He's gone to draw the trapdoor bolt! God bless them!'
>
> A jarring sound – the drop crashes down – a loud groan, sounding of hate and horror from a thousand hearts – now the shrieks and screams of women as four bodies swing in unison, heads tilted, legs twitching.
>
> Then the silence of the tomb. Justice is satisfied. Without a word the crowd slowly disperses. All is over.

But how about the victim? What was it like to be on the receiving end? Some victims were resuscitated after being hanged, others reprieved and pardoned after mishaps with faulty traps or frayed ropes.

One such was John Smith who, on 12 December 1705, was duly hanged at Tyburn. However seven minutes later, after he had been turned off, a reprieve arrived and he was cut down. Blood-letting was carried out, the universal cure in those days, and he was put in a warm bed, where eventually he recovered consciousness.

As the *Old Bailey Chronicle* reported, Smith experienced excessive pain when first turned off, but that ceased almost immediately. The last thing he remembers was an irregular and glimmering light before his eyes, and the pain he had felt earlier was nothing compared to that which he suffered when his blood started to circulate again.

Another fortunate gentleman, William Duel, was thoroughly hanged by executioner John Thrift and, cut down, was dispatched to the Surgeons' Hall for dissection. As the body was being washed preparatory to being cut open, a servant noticed that the specimen was breathing, so summoned assistance. After medical aid he 'came so much to himself as to sit up in a Chair, groan'd very much and seemed in great Agitation but could not speak', according to the *London Daily Post and General Advertiser*. When he could, however, he said that it had felt like a dream; he had been in paradise, and an angel had told him his sins were forgiven.

But perhaps the most descriptive version was given by hangman Calcraft who, after officiating at an execution at Lancaster Castle, was asked about the likely sensations experienced by his victims. His reply, quoted in a 1893 guidebook by Thomas Johnson, was:

> 'Well, I have heard it said that when you are tied up and your face turned to the Castle wall and the trap falls, you see its stones expanding and contracting violently, and a similar expansion and contraction seems to take place in your own head and breast. Then there is a rush of fire and an earthquake; your eyeballs spring out of their sockets; the Castle shoots up in the air, and you tumble down a precipice.'

Doubtless an assessment as near as anyone can get, from one who should know.

Most towns had their own gallows, but London, being the biggest city in England and therefore having the greatest number of criminals to dispose of, boasted more executions than anywhere else. Nowadays, provincial towns have their dramatic societies and repertory theatres, but if one wants to see a really big show with all the trappings and atmosphere, the 'smell of the sawdust, the roar of the crowd', London is the place. And it was just the same when it came to executions.

In the metropolis one would experience much bigger crowds, more atmosphere, louder roars and at times very malodorous sawdust. If the excursion had been well timed, one might even catch a multiple hanging, an event on which one could dine out for many months, back in one's own home town.

As described in an earlier chapter, London's main execution site was at Tyburn, near where now stands Marble Arch. During its six-hundred year existence it has been estimated that over 50,000 people were executed there. Some of its upper-class victims started out on their final journey from the Tower of London, but the vast majority were brought from Newgate Prison, the present site of the Old Bailey Central Criminal Court.

Most of the old towns were originally walled for defence, and were entered via heavily guarded and fortified gates, the gatehouses themselves being the logical places in which to secure criminals. London was no exception and its 'Newgate' became a major prison for many centuries. Disease-ridden, overcrowded, in constant need of repair, nevertheless it survived nearly every catastrophe. In 1381 it was burnt down in the Wat Tyler revolt but was rebuilt in 1422, funded by a charity left by Sir Richard Whittington, Dick Whittington of pantomime fame, though instead of a cat with one tail and nine lives, the Newgate cat had one wooden handle and nine whipcord tails. The slang name for the prison then became 'Whit's College' and the inmates were said to have 'studied at Whittington College, been examined at the Old Bailey and taken a high degree near Hyde Park Corner'.

The Great Fire of 1666 partially destroyed the prison and again it was rebuilt, though with little benefit to the prisoners. The gaoler, however, reaped a rich harvest, charging his clients for food, ale, even water. Easement of irons, that is, the removal of heavy shackles or their replacement by lighter chains, always showed a good profit, as did the provision of candles and kindling.

Digressing for a moment, it is of interest to note that not only did the early American colonists name their towns after English towns, Boston, Rochester, Plymouth and suchlike, they also named one of their chief gaols Newgate Prison. It was built on the banks of the Hudson River in Greenwich Village, near New York, and its thick and high walls surrounded blocks housing 500 inmates.

Only those sentenced to three years' imprisonment or more were sent there, and as an incentive for good work and conduct each prisoner received a daily pint of beer. In 1825 a new prison, Mount Pleasant, was built some miles away, its name later being changed to Sing Sing. The American Newgate was demolished and appropriately enough, a brewery was eventually built on the site.

London's Newgate always attracted the public's attention, especially on the Sunday preceding execution day, for they were then permitted to attend service in the prison chapel, there to study, vulture-like, those felons destined for the scaffold. The condemned prisoners themselves sat in a separate, black-draped pew, in full view of their coffins which rested on a nearby table.

None of the prison inmates got much peace the night before hanging day, at least from the year 1604, for in that year Master Robert Dow, a London merchant, grew concerned about the souls of the doomed felons. Accordingly he bequeathed £1.6s.8d a year so that the sexton, or bell-man, of St Sepulchre's Church, opposite Newgate, could guide their thoughts into Christian channels.

It is doubtful whether he succeeded, particularly among those prisoners who preferred a good night's sleep, for one part of the bequest was that the sexton should go to the prison at midnight, ring his handbell and, as loudly as possible, exhort all within to search their souls and repent their sins. Incidentally, visitors to the church will find that selfsame handbell in a small glass case attached to a pillar at the east end of the north aisle, its iron tongue now stilled.

The other requirement of Robert Dow's charity was for

the church's great bell to be tolled, twelve times with double strokes, as the grim procession left the prison on execution morning. This practice continued for 286 years until the hanging for murder of Mary Pearcey on 23 December 1890 by executioner Berry. A guest at the nearby Viaduct Hotel being ill, the vicar of St Sepulchre's was asked to cancel the bellringing, and the tradition was never renewed.

Also dispensed with was the sounding of the great bell after the victims had reached Tyburn and had been hanged. The distance, two miles between gallows and church, had always posed communication problems and at one time pigeons were released when the felons had been turned off, the birds' return to the church galvanizing the bellman into action.

To some prisoners, the very journey itself, even ending as it did at the gallows, nevertheless came as a veritable relief. Many of them were incarcerated in the dungeon named 'Limbo', in dark and fetid conditions, food being lowered in baskets to them by the gaoler, meagre rations consisting of mouldy bread and sour meat.

Those persecuted for their religious beliefs were singled out for particularly harsh treatment. Chained in an upright stance for weeks on end, iron collars about their necks, with no hope of reprieve. Only their faith sustained them during their privations.

Rarely did they have contact with the outside world. In 1537, a woman, Margaret Clements, managed to bribe the avaricious gaoler to allow her to visit monks immured in 'Limbo'. Disguised as a milkmaid, she fed them with nourishing food, having to put the morsels in their mouths because of their chained wrists.

Another pious lady, Anne Line, sheltered Venerable Father Francis Page from those who were searching her house. He managed to escape but she was captured and after sentence of death had been passed, she too was imprisoned in the filth and squalor of Newgate.

And on 27 February 1601 she was taken to Tyburn where, before the massed crowds, she proclaimed defiantly that, far from repenting, she wished with all her soul that she could have sheltered a thousand priests. Her spirit unbroken, she was subsequently martyred for her faith and fortitude.

To many, Newgate itself must have seemed like hell, but worse awaited them when execution day finally dawned and they were herded out, to set off on their journey to Tyburn.

Originally the victims were dragged there behind a horse, but since this mode of non-transport frequently resulted in the premature death of the felon before reaching his destination, thereby depriving the assembled public of the entertainment they had been waiting hours to see, with dire repercussions for the hangman and sheriff, alternative methods had to be adopted.

An ox-hide or hurdle proved rather more durable, but was later replaced by a cart. This new type of transport was ideal, in that it not only allowed more than one felon to be carried, but there was also room for the hangman, officials and the coffins, proving that time and motion studies do sometimes work.

Another advantage immediately became apparent. The ox-hide/hurdle method had meant that only the front row of the crowds lining the route to Tyburn could see the victim as the procession passed by. But the cart changed all that, for now the cortège was visible to all, and was even appreciated by the victim, allowing him to preen himself like a modern pop star, to revel in his moment of glory and accept the crowd's adulation.

And crowds there were, packing the roadsides since dawn, with here and there the gentry in carriages, complete with hampers and wine. Vendors of fruit, gingerbreads, ale and hot potatoes did a roaring trade, as did the pickpockets, albeit in a quieter fashion. At various places along the way the procession would halt for refreshments, one being at the hospital of St Giles in the Fields, where the official party were given a great bowl of wine. It is recorded, however, that one victim, spurning the offer of a drink, was forthwith taken to Tyburn and hanged. Minutes later a reprieve arrived – a dire warning to all teetotallers!

This custom, possibly the origin of the saying 'one for the

road', was discontinued in 1750, although a tavern called The Bowl was later built on the site of the old hospital.

On arrival at the gallows, the use of a cart also speeded up production (or extermination) considerably. The old method, as described earlier, required the victim to climb the ladder, whereupon the hangman's assistant, astride the beam, would tighten the noose about the felon's neck or, if the victim had already brought it with him in position, would secure the loose end to the beam. The hangman then twisted the ladder away, turning off the victim. This made the hanging of half a dozen or so felons a slow and laborious business, as it was impractical to have half a dozen ladders and the same number of assistants all swarming about and getting in each other's way on the cross-beam.

With the introduction of the new transport, the cart could be positioned beneath the beam, the unfortunates noosed almost simultaneously and all that was then required was a quick slap delivered by the hangman to the horse's flank and hey presto, the job was done in a minute.

And when in 1571, the Triple Tree replaced the old gallows, its three cross-beams could accommodate up to twenty-four victims at a time. That's progress! The crowds, somewhat aggrieved at the shortening of the advertised programme, were doubtless compensated by the spectacle of a whole troupe of corpses, all slowly gyrating together.

The nearest equivalent to the scene at Tyburn on 'collar day' would, I suppose, be Wembley Stadium on Cup Final day, a bullfight arena or a rock concert. Literally thousands packed around the scaffold for hours, balconies and grandstands full, the multitude surging and jostling as the hour grew near. Scuffles would break out as thieves were caught with their hands in the wrong pockets, and ale-women and ladies of less salubrious professions plied their wares. The scene was admirably summed up by the novelist William Makepeace Thackeray who, on attending an execution in 1840, wrote in *Fraser's Magazine* that the windows overlooking the scaffold 'were full of quiet family parties of honest tradesmen, sipping tea with calm, and moustached dandies squirting the throng below with brandy and water'.

Bawdy songs were sung, interspersed with the fifty-first psalm, which was known as the Neckverse or Tyburn Hymn, and also a revivalist song, 'Oh my, think I've got to die!' And all the time they would be listening for the distant roar which would herald the approach of the hanging procession, in much the same way as present-day spectators outside Westminster Abbey on coronation day thrill with expectation when the police urge people to keep back, and the leading coaches are heard. So it was at Tyburn, the murmur of anticipation tinged with a bloodthirsty undercurrent of excitement, growing louder and more intense, like a spark travelling along a touchpaper, to explode into a frenzy as the cart, sometimes escorted by soldiers and other officials on horseback, came into view.

All eyes were of course on the victims, who sat with their backs to the horse, nooses around their necks in readiness. Sitting facing aft meant that instead of seeing the gallows loom larger and larger during the last few hundred yards, they would not know they had actually arrived until the cart stopped beneath the cross-beam. Not so much a merciful touch, more likely a measure to prevent suddenly terror-stricken passengers from attempting to escape into the crowd.

And with the condemned, the clergy and the coffins, was the master of ceremonies himself, the Ruler of the Rope. He it was who positioned the cart, supervised his assistant, blindfolded the victims and then prodded the horse into action.

One executioner whose name comes down through judicial history, if only because his demeanour contrasted with the public image of a hangman, was John Hooper. No fearsome ogre, he could always be relied on to enliven a gallows performance with a merry grin on his ugly face, together with a bit of clowning. So much so that the crowds called him 'the laughing hangman' and 'Jolly Jack Hooper'. Nor was his humour at the expense of the victim, and so it perhaps served to alleviate their distress or even distract them in their final moments.

John Hooper's earlier career had been in the prison service, as assistant turnkey at Newgate Prison, and it was while he was escorting prisoners that he had made the acquaintance of hangman Richard Arnet. They became close friends, and when Arnet died in 1728 Hooper applied for the vacant post.

During his period of office he dealt proficiently with the routine breakers of the law, men and women alike. Some were more deserving of capital punishment than others, especially the perpetrators of a crime that shocked London in February 1733, when the bodies of three murdered women were discovered in an apartment in the Inner Temple, near Fleet Street.

One victim was an 80-year-old woman, Lydia Duncomb, the other two being her servants, Elizabeth Harrison aged sixty and Ann Price, seventeen. The two older women had been strangled and Ann's throat had been cut from ear to ear, the motive having been to steal the not inconsiderable amount of silver and money in the apartment.

Suspicion fell on Sarah Malcolm, a laundress employed by the local residents and although she tried to blame others, she was eventually tried and found guilty of the horrific crime.

In the condemned cell in Newgate she was completely unrepentant and when, at midnight on the day preceding her execution, the bellman came to exhort her to express remorse, she threw him a shilling and told him to treat himself to a pint of wine.

At dawn she put on her best clothes, rouged her cheeks carefully and then rode in the cart, treating Jolly Jack's quips with utter disdain. The law required that she be hanged outside the place of her crime, but because the Inner Temple could not accommodate a scaffold, one was erected in the middle of Fleet Street, between Mitre Court and Fetter Lane.

Such a venue provided ample space for the large number of spectators attracted by the publicity surrounding both the crime and the criminal, but Sarah ignored them completely as John Hooper positioned the noose about her neck. Within seconds he had whipped up the horse and, as the cart drew away, the rope tightened, leaving Sarah Malcolm to swing lifelessly.

Hooper's career continued until 1735 but thereafter no mention of him occurs in the gallows records. He may have retired shortly afterwards, for the post of hangman is reported to have been occupied by John Thrift early in the year. Whatever his ultimate fate, John Hooper more than any other hangman sought to brighten the last grim moments of those condemned to the gallows, and so deserves lasting credit for his gentle levity.

Later in the eighteenth century, in 1752, Thomas Turlis graced the London scaffold, a man who showed himself to be a dedicated and efficient craftsman of his trade. Unlike many of his predecessors he was educated and literate, and it is a matter for conjecture how much higher than a scaffold he could have risen, had he chosen a more favoured career.

As a hangman there were certainly many occasions when he was far from being popular with the mob, but despite bruises and brickbats he rarely retreated. His conscientiousness was in marked contrast to his predecessor John Thrift, the executioner who so tearfully wielded the axe in 1747. Upon Thrift's death, Turlis was promoted from being an assistant, to take full charge of the scaffold.

And gallows business was certainly brisk in those days, with yet another crime added to the scores already carrying the death penalty, that of forgery. Murders too were more frequent, and in order to combat the rising crime rate Parliament introduced a psychological deterrent. Aware of the repugnance felt by criminals at the thought of their bodies being cut up and dismembered after death, the Commons passed an act in Turlis's first year of office, decreeing that after hanging, all bodies were to be handed over to the Surgeons' Company for dissection. The only permissible alternative was that of gibbeting the corpse, coating it with tar and suspending it by a chain, sometimes in an iron cage, on a hill top or at cross-roads.

Although the crime wave brought more income to Turlis, who was paid as always on commission in addition to his fixed retaining wage, the Dissection Act immediately increased the risk to his life and limb. His was the responsibility of cutting down the bodies and giving them to the medics, and this was challenged by the victims' friends and relatives. Indeed, on 18 December 1758 some surgeons asserted their right to a corpse and a riot broke out, injuring several people. The mob eventually won and carried the now sadly dishevelled corpse away in triumph.

Turlis's performances were not always as dramatic as that, of course. Many routine hangings were carried out without any disturbance and he was often kept busy, there being times when he had to dispatch as many as twelve felons in a day.

In 1759 a small landmark in the history of Tyburn occurred. For over six hundred years the gallows had been a fixture there, a structure to warn and terrify by its very presence all who passed along Watling Street. But even as today, when thoroughfares have to be widened to cope with increased traffic, so the Tree impeded the flow of coaches and wagons, cattle and carts.

The permanent structure was therefore taken down and replaced by a portable version which was assembled and dragged into position when required. Or, as the *Whitehall Evening Post* phrased it: 'Yesterday morning, about Half an Hour after Nine o'clock, the four malefactors were carried in two carts from Newgate and executed on the new Moving Gallows at Tyburn. After the Bodies were cut down, the Gallows were carried off in a cart.' The site of the old gallows was later occupied by a new toll gate, a structure detested by travellers almost as much as had been the gallows!

Even the site of the portable version was apt to vary, depending on the influence of the local residents. One such was the Dowager Lady Waldegrave who, as reported in the *Gazetteer* of 4 May 1771, 'was having a grand house built near Tyburn, and through the particular interest of her Ladyship, the place of execution will be moved to another spot'.

New as the portable gallows were, further innovations were to follow, for in the following year Turlis, Tyburn and the Tower combined to present a spectacle, the like of which would never be seen again – nothing less than the hanging of a peer of the realm!

Laurence Shirley, Earl Ferrers, was noted for his eccentric ways and violent behaviour, characteristics which were tolerated until, on 18 January 1760, he quarrelled with Johnson, his estate agent, and fatally shot him.

After his arrest he was confined in the Tower of London, where, incidentally, his grandfather had been born. The Earl was held in the Middle Tower, an outer bastion well known to the author when on duty beneath its archway. Earl Ferrers was one of the very few prisoners ever housed therein, the Middle Tower being too near the castle's perimeter to be completely escape-proof, so reports of ghostly footsteps on its battlements have consequently been attributed to the paranoic Earl.

He was heavily guarded, two yeoman warders being in the room with him and another at the door. Two soldiers were stationed at the foot of the spiral stairs and a further guard stood on the drawbridge, all with fixed bayonets. The Earl ate well while in captivity, his breakfast consisting of a half-pint basin of tea with a small spoonful of brandy in it, and a muffin. With his dinner he drank a pint of wine and a pint of water, and another pint of each with his supper.

As befitted his rank he was tried before the House of Lords and, being found guilty, was condemned to death. His plea, as a peer of the realm, to be executed by the axe on Tower Hill, was rejected and he was sentenced to be hanged and then anatomized. A further plea, that he should be hanged by a silken rope, by virtue of his rank, was similarly refused, one reason being that there was insufficient time in which to have one woven.

In the Tower he gave no trouble and indeed played cards for money with his warders, though they refused to play every night! And on the morning of 5 May 1760 he got dressed in a white satin suit embroidered with silver lace, looking every inch the star of one of the most magnificent cavalcades ever to have left the Tower since the coronation processions of earlier days.

Behind Grenadier Guards and lines of marching constables, coaches carried the sheriffs and other officials, their horses decked with black ribbons. The Earl had his own personal landau drawn by six horses, the coachman of which, it is reported, cried all the way! The hearse followed, with mourning coaches full of friends, and a company of Life Guards brought up the rear. So packed were the streets that the procession took two and three-quarter hours to cover the three miles to Tyburn, for a peer had never suffered there before, and no Londoner worthy of his, or her, salt would want to miss an event like that.

On the way the Earl chewed tobacco and leant out of the window to wave to the crowds, and when the horse of an escorting dragoon caught a leg in the carriage wheel and threw its rider, Ferrers expressed much concern, exclaiming 'I hope there will be no death today but mine!'

Forcing its way through the crush, the procession eventually reached Tyburn, where Turlis waited by the newly invented machine which was ultimately to revolutionize the art of the hangman. Improved and finally adopted by 1783, this particular day in 1760 was its first trial with a human being, and so who better than a real lord from the Tower of London?

The new device consisted of a heavy horizontal beam mounted between two posts. A platform was sited beneath the structure and a section of it, about three feet square and covered in black baize, was raised about eighteen inches above the rest of the flooring. Earl Ferrers was led on to the small platform, there to kneel on black cushions and pray. Rising at last, he presented the sheriff with his watch, and the chaplain with five guineas. It was then that the solemn ritual was rudely shattered as the Earl, understandably ignorant of the Ketch pecking order, gave five guineas not to Turlis but to his assistant, a man whose name has not come down to us. But names there were in plenty as a furious row broke out between the two, Turlis eventually getting possession of the money.

He then prepared the Earl by tying the man's hands in front of him with a black sash – cords were for commoners – and, guiding his victim on to the raised part of the platform, positioned the noose about the Earl's neck. As the Earl asked, 'Am I right?' Turlis nodded and pulled a white cap down over the victim's face. A brief pause, and then the executioner operated the mechanism, causing the flooring on which the Earl stood, to drop.

It was immediately apparent that although it was an improvement in principle, the device was far from being a success. As the renowned author Horace Walpole, Earl of Orford wrote:

> As the machine was new, they were not ready at it; his toes still touched the stage and he suffered a little, having had time, by their bungling, to raise his cap; but the executioner pulled it down again, and they pulled his legs so that he was soon out of pain, and quite dead in four minutes.

So slow strangulation was still the order of the day, albeit mechanically caused.

In accordance with the law the Earl's body had to hang for an hour, but that was no reason why people had to stand around wasting their time. So the sheriff and his fellow officials sat on the scaffold and partook of refreshments, oblivious to the pinioned corpse suspended only feet away from their table.

At long last Turlis cut the body down, a two-man job of course, one to take the weight, the other to sever the rope, and this task triggered off yet another unseemly squabble. Ever mindful of the value of the day's booty, the ownership of the halter was briskly disputed. Or, as Walpole commented, 'The executioners fought for the rope, and the one who lost it, cried!' I'll bet it wasn't Turlis! Nor were the crowd to be denied, for they tore the black baize cloth to shreds in their scramble for souvenirs.

The Earl's body was conveyed with great pomp to the Surgeons' Hall where, after incisions and dissection, it was exhibited to the general public for three days before being buried.

In dire need of modification the new-style scaffold was immediately withdrawn from use and did not make its reappearance until 1783 at the new execution site outside Newgate Prison. Perhaps disillusioned by the failure of the new model, Thomas Turlis reverted to the tried and tested method using his horse and cart, and business went on as before at Tyburn.

But one piece of business he could well have done without concerned a veritable virago called Hannah Dagoe. Hannah, a well-built Irish woman, had been caught robbing a neighbour and was promptly sentenced to death. In prison she terrorized the turnkeys and fellow convicts until, on 4 May 1763, she travelled with Turlis to the gallows.

As the cart stopped beneath the beam Hannah, with a superhuman effort, suddenly tore her hands free and attacked the hangman, raining blows to his head and shoulders. Before he could overpower her, she had torn off her hat and cloak, throwing them to the wildly cheering crowd, thereby depriving Turlis of his rightful dues.

Somehow he managed to pinion her again and then got the noose about her neck. The cap was quickly pulled down over her head, yet before he could climb out of the cart and whip the horse up, the struggling woman suddenly hurled herself over the side and died instantly of a broken neck.

Executions of evil women were always crowd-pullers at Tyburn, the most notorious being Elizabeth Brownrigg, a midwife who, rather then engage servants, employed a number of orphans as apprentices. Cruel in the extreme, she would horsewhip them mercilessly, giving them little food and confining them in cold and filthy cellars. So appalling was their treatment that one, Mary Clifford, died of her wounds and Elizabeth Brownrigg was deservedly condemned to death.

At her execution at Tyburn on 14 September 1767 the onlookers expressed their feelings, abuse and jeering rising to deafening cheers as Turlis's whip came down on the horse's flank and poor Mary Clifford was avenged.

Elizabeth's corpse was handed over to the surgeons for medical research and afterwards 'her skeleton was exposed in the niche opposite the first floor in the Surgeons' Theatre, that the heinousness of her cruelty may make the more lasting impression on the minds of the spectators', as the *Gentleman's Magazine* noted.

Less than a year later an almost identical crime was perpetrated when Sarah Metyard and her daughter Morgan were charged with the brutal murder of one of their five parish apprentices. The body had been cut up, the pieces scattered around the neighbourhood, and it was not until several years later that the daughter confessed. Both were executed, the hanging of Sarah causing particular problems for Thomas Turlis. The *Newgate Calendar* described how; 'the mother, being in a fit when she was put into the cart, she lay at her length till she came to the place of execution, when she was raised up, and means were used for her recovery but without effect, so that she departed this life in a state of unsensibility'. To support an unconscious person, even with the aid of an assistant, whilst setting the halter around their neck, says much for Turlis's intensity of purpose. It was also a painless end for the victim!

Tyburn did not have all the interesting executions, of course. Sometimes the hanging procession headed towards the East End rather than the west, making for Wapping, to Execution Dock at the river's edge. Hangings at this site were exclusively reserved for crimes which had been committed at sea, pirates, mutineers, brutal captains and the like. As they could not be hanged at the scene of their crime, they met their end as near to it as possible, and Execution Dock had been the designated site for hundreds of years. As Machyn relates in his *Diary*, '1557 the vi day of Aprell was hangyd at the low-water marke at Wapyng be-yond St Katheryn's, vii men for robbing on the see'.

The low-water mark was part of the grim ceremony, for after the nautical felon had been hanged on the gallows erected on the shore, the body was chained to a stake at the low-water mark, where it was left for three high tides. The purpose of this was as a deterrent. Had the bodies been gibbeted on hill tops or displayed over the City gates, other potential pirates would not have seen them. Exhibited, however, within sight of the hundreds of ships entering and leaving the Port of London, they acted as a horrific reminder. It was reported in *Old and New London* of March 1874 that in 1816 Mr Townsend, a notable Bow Street Runner, gave evidence on crime and policing in the House of Commons. Being in favour of such visible deterrents, he said that he was against the present law whereby some hanged mariners were afterwards dissected and done away with.

> 'But look at this,' he went on. 'There are a couple of men now hanging near the Thames, where all the sailors must sail past; and one sailor says to the other "Pray what are those two poor fellows there for?" "Why" says another, "I will go and ask." They ask. "Why, these two men are hung and gibbeted for murdering His Majesty's revenue officers." And so the warning is kept alive.'

Nor were such executions isolated occurrences. Paul Hentzner, international traveller in the sixteenth century, wrote that 300 pirates were hanged in London each year.

So when Captain David Ferguson, master of the merchant ship *Betsey*, was arrested for the murder of his cabin boy whilst *en route* from Virginia, he was tried at the Admiralty Sessions at the Old Bailey. The crime was extremely brutal, as was Ferguson's treatment of his crew, and he received the death sentence.

On the fateful day, 4 January 1771, the procession left Newgate, but this time wended its way east through Cheapside and Cornhill, past Leadenhall Market and Tower Hill to the bend of the river at Wapping.

The East Enders had turned out in full force, packing every available viewpoint, the riverside taverns and jetties being jammed with spectators. Off shore, lines of barges accommodated those who could afford such sought-after places, and further out in the river, ships were anchored, their decks and rigging swarming with yet more of the curious, the cynical or the morbid.

Nor was it just the execution that attracted them, for the procession itself was a sight to behold. It was led by the Deputy Marshal of the Admiralty carrying the Silver Oar, symbol of the jurisdiction that that court held over all mariners. He was followed by the Marshal of the Admiralty resplendent in his traditional uniform, his coachmen wearing their distinctive livery, and behind came the City marshals on horseback. The vehicle that caused the real hum of excitement was of course the cart carrying Captain Ferguson, Thomas Turlis and the Newgate clergyman, this being heavily escorted by the sheriff's men, mounted and on foot.

Once at the Thames shore the procedure was brief. The sea captain was led down from the wharf to the beach, to stand on the platform beneath the gallows beam. Prayers were said and the noose placed around the neck of the victim who was then blindfolded. The assistant hangman, taking his place on the cross-beam, waited until Turlis had guided his charge up the ladder, and he then secured the rope tightly to the beam. As a deathly hush fell over the massed onlookers, Turlis reached out and, with an expert twist of his wrists, turned the ladder away, leaving the felon to die.

After the requisite delay, the executioner and his assistant lowered the body and chained it to the wooden stake driven deep into the muddy sands, its head and limbs to loll with the tides as a grim warning to all on the high seas.

There was another occasion during that January when sea and sand had connections with Turlis's executions, for three days before Wapping he had hanged John Clark and John Joseph Defoe at Tyburn, both having been found guilty of robbery. And Joseph Defoe, it was said, was the grandson of Daniel Defoe, the author of the book *Robinson Crusoe*.

The year 1771 marked the end of Turlis's career and indeed his life. On 27 March he was involved in a scuffle with his prisoners at Tyburn. This was not an unusual happening, and the executions were carried out without further trouble. But Turlis must have sustained injuries not immediately apparent, for a few days later, whilst returning from another execution, he collapsed in the cart and died. A fitting end for a professional hangman.

After his death scaffold life went on as usual, under new management, the boss being Edward Dennis, a man who dealt quite adequately with his clientele of thieves and murderers, coiners and highwaymen. Reliable and unimaginative, he and his assistant worked well together, a partnership that was threatened in 1780 when the Gordon Riots broke out.

Lord Gordon, a fanatical Protestant, had whipped public opinion to fever pitch in his campaign to oppress the Roman Catholics, and inevitably the orderly demonstrations turned into a full-scale riot. Mobs, hundreds strong, surged through the streets, burning and looting. Houses and shops in Drury Lane and Holborn were broken into and pillaged, coaches were stopped and their passengers violently assaulted by hooligans wielding bludgeons, chisels, even the spokes of cart wheels. Catholic chapels were desecrated, prisons set on fire, the prisoners being helped to escape, and when the Bank of England came under attack the Horseguards and Footguards were called out to protect public buildings.

The King set up an operations control room in the Queen's Riding House and involved himself in the efforts to bring the situation to order, and 11,000 soldiers were assembled in St James's and Hyde Parks, some guarding Buckingham House, with fixed bayonets to be used if necessary.

On the third evening of the riot Ned Dennis, *en route* to his house in Newtoner Street (now Newton Street) off High Holborn, was suddenly caught up in a mob wrecking a chandler's shop. Before he realized what he was doing, and doubtless spurred on by the frenzy of those around him, he found himself taking part, smashing windows and hurling furniture into the street.

Some of his fellow rioters recognized him and, his name later reaching the authorities, he was arrested. The fact that the London hangman was involved in the disturbances was eagerly seized on by the newspapers, the *St James's Chronicle* of 13 June commenting: 'On Monday night the Person commonly called Jack Ketch was apprehended at the sign of the Blue Posts, an Ale House in Southampton Buildings, Holborn, on Suspicion of being a Ringleader in the late Riots.'

At his trial Dennis broke down completely, begging for mercy, but the evidence was irrefutable, and he was sentenced to death. In prison, the Tothillfields Bridewell, he was kept apart from the other convicts for his own safety, and there he resigned himself to the fate he knew so well.

While awaiting his execution he requested the authorities to allow his son to succeed him as hangman, a suggestion which, as pointed out by a journalist, would require a son to hang his own father! The eventuality, however, did not arise. Many rioters had been rounded up and had to be punished. Edward Dennis was needed to apply the penalties and so was reprieved in order that he could hang his fellow rioters.

And hang them he did, at various places throughout the City, in Bow Street and Bunhill Row, Bishopsgate and Bloomsbury Square. Others met their end in Oxford Road, Whitechapel and Old Street, a veritable travelling circus.

It is highly probable that he officiated at the hanging, in June 1780, of Mary Roberts, Charlotte Gardiner and William M'Donald, three rioters who thus had the unwelcome honour of being the last persons to be executed on Tower Hill, where so many aristocratic prisoners from the Tower of London had perished.

Dennis's alleged role as a ringleader was exaggerated, but earned him a place in English literature, for sixty years later he was portrayed as such in *Barnaby Rudge*, a novel by Charles Dickens, based on the memories of men and women who had lived through those turbulent times.

Dennis's own close brush with death would seem to have upset his usual efficiency, for in the months that followed, he bungled several executions and was the target of much abuse from the Tyburn crowds. However, he settled down again and, with his assistant Brunskill, continued to rule the gallows.

The two men, though, were soon to lose their long-established headquarters, for after six centuries the days of the Tyburn gallows were finally numbered. Just as nowadays, when the developers move in and alter entire neighbourhoods, so in the eighteenth century the affluent citizens of London were vacating the inner city and moving out into the suburbs. And as a residence overlooking the gallows could hardly be classed as a desirable property by even the most smooth-tongued estate agent, let alone having one's front garden frequently invaded by a frenzied mêlée of gallows ghouls, Tyburn had to go.

And so, on 7 November 1783, the last hanging took place there, that of robber John Austin. Dennis, or perhaps Brunskill, bungled it somewhat, for the halter slipped round to the back of Austin's neck and prolonged his death unnecessarily.

The new site adopted by the authorities was the convenient one of Newgate Prison itself, new gallows being built just outside the prison walls. The Tyburn area, at last rid of its ghastly gatherings, also sought to expunge its evil reputation. Eventually Tyburn Road was renamed Oxford Street, Tyburn Lane became Park Lane and Tyburn Gate was changed to Cumberland Gate. But in Hyde Park Place the old name still survives, Tyburn Convent being a lasting reminder of the 105 Carthusians, Benedictines, Jesuits and many others who, between 1535 and 1681, lost their lives nearby. Revered with other relics are some of the timbers of the ancient scaffold, although much of the demolished structure was acquired by a local innkeeper for use as barrel stands.

Following the move to Newgate, Dennis and his assistant were soon in action at the new premises. On 9 December 1783 they achieved the feat of hanging ten convicts simultaneously, this being made possible by gallows of an improved design.

This took the form of a black-covered scaffold, a six-foot high platform in which was a large hatch, ten feet long by eight feet wide. At each end of the hatch a stout upright supported two parallel cross-beams from which the ropes, and the victims, would hang. A lever similar to a pump handle operated the draw-bar under the trapdoors of the hatch, allowing them to fall and so plunge the victims into the pit beneath.

The prisoners were brought on to the platform via steps which led up from the prison basement, their approach being hidden by a screen so that to the waiting multitude they appeared as if on to a theatre stage. To one side seats were arranged for the sheriff and other officials, witnesses to the execution of the Law.

In theory this new, more mechanical method should have reduced the suffering of the victims but in practice the ropes were still too short, the felons falling only two or three feet, and no allowance being made for their individual weight, age, muscular development, and so on. It would be another ninety years before merciful consideration was given to such vital factors.

The two beams could accommodate up to twenty felons and indeed occasionally did so. On 2 February 1785 Dennis and Brunskill achieved that number, and of the twenty, five had been convicted for the 'serious' crime of robbing a man of two glass drops worth threepence, a one-inch ruler – twopence, two papers of nails – a penny, two shillings in coins and a counterfeit halfpenny; total value: two shillings and sevenpence, excluding the dud coin. Life, and death, was cheap in those days.

The Newgate gallows proved a great success, providing a somewhat more merciful death for its victims, though it lacked popularity with the public for they missed the grand processions through the streets from Newgate to Tyburn, and the vast arena surrounding the old gallows site, reminiscent of a Roman amphitheatre. At Newgate the victims were brought out and hardly paraded at all, before being hanged, whilst the public area was much restricted by the surrounding houses, a limitation welcomed by the sheriff and his constables.

Dennis did not have long in which to enjoy the better conditions there for, after a brief illness, he died on

Tuesday 21 November 1786. A public figure to the end, his obituary appeared in the *Daily Universal Register*, the forerunner of *The Times*, its sentiments tinged with somewhat unseemly humour:

> Yesterday died at his apartments in the Old Bailey, as regretted in death as he was respected through life, Mr Dennis, commonly called Jack Ketch. In his office of Finisher of the Law, Surveyor of the New Drop and Apparitor of the Necklace, alias Yeoman of the Halter etc. he acquitted himself with the approbation of all but the parties concerned. He had frequently a numerous company at his levee, though all complained of a want of variety in his dish, which was hearty-choak and caper sauce.

Many friends, among them his long-time assistant William Brunskill, attended his funeral, and he was buried in the graveyard of St Giles in the Fields, London, on 26 November 1786.

Not all hangings took place in the south of England, of course, nor should it be assumed, because of executioners as harsh as Ketch, Price or Dun, that London had the monopoly of such calibre of hangmen. The north of England, never noted for its namby-pambies, could callously boast that if you wanted real brutality, Edward Barlow, 'Old Ned', was your man.

Fittingly enough he was the hangman of Lancaster, a place known as the 'hanging town' because of the little faith its judges had in sentences that did not include the blindfold and the noose. Nor was this just a rumour to impress the gullible, for the county records reveal that between the years 1782 and 1835 no fewer than 256 criminals were hanged outside the city's castle.

For most of that period the Lord of the Lancaster Scaffold was Ned Barlow. He was 'as vile a rogue as ever lived', said one contemporary historian, and John Hall in his book *Lancaster Castle, its History and Associations*, published in 1843, wrote of Barlow:

> this man led a wretched life; there were very few houses into which he was permitted to enter. He was ever the butt

of scorn for all persons; many times he was seriously abused, often pelted with missiles of the foulest description. Not unfrequently was he rolled in the mud, and as often much worse treated in a nameless manner. Yet this wretch maintained his horrible post with little intermission during a period of thirty years.

Old Ned was born in Wales in 1736, but nothing is known of his earlier life before he became Lancaster's hangman in 1781. This was probably a semi-official appointment for he was not sworn in until 1786. He soon became notorious throughout the county for his ruthless treatment of those he hanged, although he was known to boast of the neatness with which he performed his job. Never one to keep a low profile, he often claimed that 'he had rid the world of many a rogue, and saved the life of one honest man', the latter being a drowning man he had once rescued.

Lancaster's Tyburn was its castle, a grim fortress brooding menacingly over the town below. Over the centuries, towers and ramparts were added to the original Norman keep, and its ancient walls have witnessed many sieges and battles. As befits its importance, many kings have stayed there – King John, Edward II, John of Gaunt, Henry IV. Edward IV took refuge in the castle, and James I visited it in 1617.

Like many old castles it was, and indeed still is a prison, and courts have been held there since 1176. The infamous Judge Jeffries once sat in session there, and many trials resulted in the executions of Catholic priests, abbots and even witches. George Fox, the Quaker, was held in one of its dungeons, and many prisoners were transported to the colonies from the castle, their leg-irons and manacles now forming a remarkable museum within the battlemented walls.

Ned Barlow was of course very familiar with all this. As hangman it was part of his job to brand convicted felons when ordered by the judge, and the branding iron he used is still on display in the richly panelled courtroom. The felon's left hand was secured in the 'holdfast', double iron grips attached to the wall of the dock, and the red-hot iron bearing the appropriate letter, 'V' for vagabond, 'M' for malefactor and so on, would be pressed against the base of the thumb. Having then inspected the smoking flesh, Old Ned would turn to the judge and proclaim 'A fair mark, my lord!'. Doubtless he was quite disappointed when in 1811 the use of the branding iron was discontinued. Other duties included wielding the whip and cat-o'-nine-tails on those pedlars and adulterers sentenced to be whipped out of town, a task which he reputedly relished.

Barlow's main theatre of operation however was in the 'drop room' of the castle. Brought into here from the prison chapel, the felons were pinioned and prepared for their execution. In the outer wall of the drop room there were, and still are, large double doors, their upper halves being glazed. These doors opened inwards, to reveal a six-foot drop to the ground outside, and this outer area, being a recess in the castle wall, was known as 'hanging corner'.

Originally a beam projected above the doors so that the victim, secured to the beam by a rope, would then be pushed out, to hang until dead. The body would then be lowered and swung back in via an opening immediately below the drop room doors into a cellar where the coffin awaited. Internal access to this lower room was obtained through a trapdoor in the floor of the drop room.

The arrangement was later modified, and gallows were erected outside, in the hanging corner. These consisted of two stout posts which fitted into square holes in two large circular stones set in the ground. The cross-beam between them could accommodate more than one felon at a time, and in fact the greatest number was eleven, in March 1801. Rather than give himself the extra work of hanging them in two or more batches, Barlow crowded them all on at once, like jackets in a wardrobe, 'resulting in a poor drop, some feet touching the ground', the old records report. Afterwards some of the bodies were buried beneath the two Sebastopol cannon which once stood on the lawns fronting the courtroom, but the vast majority of the castle's victims were interred only yards from hanging corner, below the wall which skirts the nearby parish church of St Mary.

That low wall and all the surrounding area provided vantage points for the crowds who came from all over Lancashire and Westmorland, as many as 6,000 attending a 'popular' execution. To keep a space clear for the hangman, six-foot high spiked railings were erected across the recess of hanging corner, the spectators at the very front having a ringside view, since the railings were only four yards from where it was all happening on the gallows.

One occasion when the ghoulish gathering was disappointed was on 1 October 1791. James Burns, sentenced to death, had had his leg-irons struck off by the prison black-smith, as was the practice on execution morning, and was left in the condemned cell to await an escort to the chapel. During that time he managed to commit suicide, thereby thwarting Old Ned and the gallows.

But a felon, even though dead, was not entitled to deprive the public of the drama they had come so far to see, and so the officials led a procession up on to the Moor outside the city, where the corpse was duly buried 'with a stake run through it', as the *Lancaster Guardian* reported.

Such was Barlow's callous attitude to his victims that great public satisfaction greeted the news when the tables were finally turned. After so many years of handing out barbaric punishments, Old Ned stood in the dock on criminal charges, and faced the judge in a packed courtroom.

He was accused of stealing a horse from one Peter Wright, and the case was written up in the *Lancaster Gazette* of 22 March 1806: 'Edward Barlow aged 69 years, who has been the executioner for this county for twenty years, during which time he has officiated upon eighty four criminals; for stealing a chestnut gelding, the property of P. Wright of North Meols – Guilty!'

At this verdict, which carried the death penalty, Old Ned remarked fatalistically: 'All this comes of a man getting out of his line!' The public however were to be deprived of seeing the hated hangman swing on his own gallows, for the authorities, faced with the problem that repeatedly occurred all over the country, namely how to replace a hanged hangman, interceded on Ned's behalf. His sentence was commuted to a somewhat unusual but essentially practical one, whereby he was given a ten-year gaol sentence in Lancaster Castle, but allowed to leave the prison for the purpose of performing hangings and floggings!

Segregated from the other prisoners, and probably enjoying more comfortable quarters than they, Barlow must have found that 'living over the shop' was, if anything, an improvement in his lodging arrangements, but he was not destined to serve his full sentence for after six years – and forty-seven hangings – he died in his cell, an event chronicled by the *Lancaster Gazette* of 12 December 1812:

> Died, on Wednesday last, in our castle, aged 76, Edward Barlow, alias Old Ned, alias Jack Ketch, which last situation he has filled for 31 years, during which time he has executed 131 unfortunate criminals. He was convicted of horse stealing at the March Assizes 1806 and received sentence of death but was afterwards reprieved on condition of being imprisoned for ten years.

The day after his death on 9 December 1812 he was buried in the graveyard of St Mary's parish church. Only a matter of yards, and the wall mentioned earlier, separated him from those whose lives he had ended at hanging corner.

At about the same time as Old Ned was reigning at Lancaster, John Curry was lording it over the scaffold on the other side of the Pennines, in Yorkshire. A character just as well known in the north as Barlow, he served from 1802 until 1831 and so could well have been on duty on 20 March 1809 when Mary Bateman was hanged at York. Mary had left her job as housemaid, to set up business as a fortune-teller in Leeds, combining her art with that of extorting money and property from her clients as the price of looking into their future.

The greed of the 'Yorkshire Witch', as she became known, led her to commit murder and she was hanged at the new drop behind York Castle. Thousands attended her final moments, many believing that as a witch with supernatural powers she would vanish at the very moment when the rope grew taut. But when it did – she didn't!

Back in Leeds, twenty-three miles away, a crowd of nearly 2,500 had paid threepence each to view the body on its return and they waited more or less patiently until the hearse arrived at midnight. The proceeds of the morbid exhibition, £30 in total, swelled the coffers of the Leeds General Infirmary, where the body was later dissected.

In accordance with a local custom at that time, her skin was tanned and distributed in small pieces to those who applied and, as reported in the *Folklore of Yorkshire*, published in 1901, parts of her skin were still on sale in Ilkley as late as 1892. Doubtless the witch's remains were advertised in the appropriately named magazine.

Meanwhile down south, William Brunskill was busy dispatching London's felons. Unusually, Brunskill was a sober and conscientious man and, having been an assistant hangman for twelve years, was as competent as could be expected when he took over in 1786. Whatever claim to fame he had, however, occurred on 18 May 1812, for only a week earlier the Prime Minister, Spencer Perceval, on entering the House of Commons, had been fatally shot by John Bellingham, a bankrupt Liverpool broker who bore a grudge against the government.

Little time was wasted in bringing the assassin to justice, no lengthy trial or appeal being allowed to prolong the judicial proceedings, for Bellingham was found guilty and led to the scaffold three days later.

Despite the heavy rain many celebrities were present in the packed Newgate arena, among them the poet Lord Byron and the radical essayist and politician William Cobbett. Many in the crowd demonstrated their opinion of the government by cheering Bellingham and hurling abuse at Brunskill, but such receptions were all in a day's work to a hangman, and the execution took place without undue incident.

Brunskill's thirty-eight years of executions were by now telling on him, a strain suffered eventually by most hangmen. He had had to work in all weathers and despite being a hard and honest worker, his job had made him the target of public hostility and odium whenever he appeared on the scaffold. Nor was his pay any consolation. A small retaining wage was meant to be augmented by payment for each execution and whipping, but Brunskill was in office at an unprofitable time for hangmen. War with the French meant that the criminal elements finished up in the ranks of the army rather than on the scaffold. And the earlier decision of the government to transport offenders to Australia instead of in the cart to Tyburn, further reduced Brunskill's income.

By 1814 he was frail and infirm, every hanging calling for ever greater efforts. In November that year he suffered a stroke and so John Langley, his faithful assistant for the last twenty-four years, took over. A few months later, in May 1815, Brunskill submitted his resignation to the City aldermen, the letter still being preserved in the Guildhall Record Office. He was granted a pension of fifteen shillings a week, adequate enough for those days, and he died peacefully in his bed a year or so later.

Little is known of Langley's personality. In the shadow of Brunskill for nearly a quarter of a century, he held the limelight for just two and a half years, dying at the age of fifty-one.

His successor, James Botting, a coarse, insensitive man, had been assistant to Langley in 1814 for the princely sum of ten shillings and sixpence a week, but eventually took over in 1817. In that year a sailor, Thomas Cashman, and others were members of a radical socialist society called the Spencean movement formed by a Yorkshire school-master named Spence. On 2 December 1816 they held a public meeting in Spa Fields in London and, doubtless inspired by the French assault on the Bastille and the ensuing overthrow of the hated aristocracy, the agitators marched in procession to the Tower of London, where they demanded the surrender of the garrison.

Being greeted with laughter (and probably urged to get into the ticket queue) by the yeoman warders and sentries, the crowd surged back into the City, where they ransacked a gun shop. Troops were called in to disperse the mob, some leaders being held in the Tower, and one of them, Thomas Cashman, was sentenced to death.

On 12 March 1817 he was duly hanged in Skinner Street, Snow Hill, by James Botting and John Langley. The condemned man's supporters turned up in full force and it was only the protection provided by the soldiers and constables that allowed the two hangmen to get away without serious injury. But if you hand it out, you have to be prepared to take it, and surly James Botting was well equipped to run the risks of his calling.

As the years went by, the stressful life took its toll of the hangman. He suffered a stroke and, unable to work, had to retire. Later, crippled by paralysis, he could only hobble about the streets, before being confined to his room in Brighton. But his doughty spirit kept him going until his death on 1 October 1837.

One of the all-time greats among the ranks of English hangmen now ascended the scaffold steps – William Calcraft by name, famous if only for the length of his reign and the shortness of his rope – forty-five years for the former, about three feet for the latter. A simple, unimaginative man, it never occurred to him that his 'short drop' killed his victims by slow and agonizing strangulation. Or maybe he did not stop to think that there could be any other way.

Occasionally he would seek to expedite his victim's demise as best he could. The novelist William Makepeace Thackeray, present at one of Calcraft's performances, described how the hangman 'came up from his black hole and, seizing the prisoner's legs, pulled on them until he was quite dead – strangled!'

Calcraft kept his favourite ropes in a canvas bag, some of which he had used for twenty years or more on scaffolds all over the country. One drop chain and noose still survives in Lancaster Castle, the author being able to vouch for its short length of less than three feet, and this particular rope was used by Calcraft to hang Richard Pedder, who had murdered his wife on 29 August 1857.

One innovation introduced by Calcraft was a belt, a

harness of black straps complete with buckles, with which to secure his captive's wrists. He is quoted in an old guidebook as saying 'It's my own invention. The old pinions used to hurt the old fellows so. This waist strap answers [fits] every person and is not in the least uncomfortable.'

It could be said that the death of William Calcraft in 1879 marked the end of an era of relative inhumanity on the scaffold, for the next to mount the steps was William Marwood, in 1871, who first executed a prisoner in Lincoln Gaol, before later moving south to London. Just why he developed an interest in hanging is not known. The melodramatic accounts of executions in the local newspapers could well have troubled his conscience, or perhaps the sheer mechanics of the operation appealed to his innovative nature. Whatever the reason, he eventually perfected the 'long drop' method, in which the victim fell a carefully calculated distance of between six and ten feet, thereby drastically reducing the suffering endured by those condemned to death.

The length of the rope would depend on the felon's weight and other factors such as age and muscular development. 'Weigh carefully and give as long a drop as possible', was his maxim. If gauged correctly the drop, or more precisely the abrupt tightening of the rope, would cause fracture dislocation of the neck's vertebrae, pressure on, or severing of the spinal cord and medulla, and so cause instant death.

Credit must be given to this rural cobbler who, lacking medical training, introduced scientific calculation and thereby mercy into the callous business of executions. One wonders how he confirmed its efficacy without volunteers!

When appointed hangman, he performed his duties in a humane and conscientious manner, proud of his own ability. The public respected him, an achievement rarely earned by any of his profession, and he regarded himself as an important government official, letting it be known that his title was 'executioner', not 'hangman'. His cobbler's shop displayed a sign 'Crown Office' and customers bringing shoes for repair could also study the nooses Marwood had used on some of his more famous victims. With the ropes hung one of Calcraft's cruelly short ropes in harsh contrast. 'He HANGED them,' Marwood would exclaim scathingly, 'I EXECUTE them!'

By this time crimes carrying the death penalty had been so reduced in number that provincial hangings were performed by the London hangman. But despite having to travel all over the country, Marwood still found time to devise improvements to his equipment. He is generally credited with replacing the 'hangman's knot' with a metal ring, ensuring a smoother and more rapid tightening of the noose.

His new methods were not successful every time, however, some hangings giving a grim twist to the phrase 'trial and error'. One of them was the execution of Mark Fiddler, or Fidler, at Lancaster Castle on 16 August 1875, which almost ended in disaster. Absent were the crowds who had flocked to previous executions, for this one was the first to be held in private there, taking place in the relative seclusion of the chapel yard.

Fiddler had previously attempted to commit suicide by cutting his throat, and the official witnesses were shocked on seeing that the long drop, although calculated accurately by Marwood, had nevertheless ruptured the partially healed wound in the victim's throat. Had the drop been longer, the result could well have resulted in a horrifying decapitation.

Such near tragedies doubtless upset the executioner considerably, for like many Victorians he was deeply religious. In the Crown Court of Lancaster Castle there was until recent years a copy of the Testament, its flyleaf signed 'Wm. Marwood July 15 1867', which was probably the one that he carried round with him on his hanging circuit. The pinioning strap used by him, a three-inch wide body strap with two wrist straps attached, is still on display there.

Although by then all executions were carried out behind prison walls, William Marwood was well known to the public through newspaper accounts of hangings, many of which included pictures of him. In appearance he resembled many another respectable Victorian gentleman, in his high-collared black coat with tails and side pockets. He often wore a low felt hat on his thinning grey hair, and he kept his small moustache and mutton-chop sideburns neatly trimmed. When off duty he would smoke a pipe and partake of his favourite drink of gin and water.

On duty of course he dispatched many infamous criminals, murderers such as Vincent Walker, Fenian Joe Brady and Charles Peace. But perhaps the most gruesome murder was on 5 March 1879 when a box washed up by the Thames at Hammersmith was found to contain large pieces of boiled flesh.

The remains were identified as those of a Mrs Thomas who lived in Richmond, and on investigating, the police discovered that the contents of the Thomas household had been advertised for sale by Mrs Thomas's servant, a thirty-year old Irish woman called Kate Webster. A thorough search after the servant's arrest disclosed the full enormity of the hideous crime. Not only had Kate killed her employer, but had then dismembered the corpse and boiled various limbs in the steam boiler in the house.

Rumours abounded, some to the effect that in order to dispose of other damning evidence, she had hidden the head – which was never found – and had even sold jars of human dripping to inns in the neighbourhood! The result of her trial was a foregone conclusion, and at Wandsworth later in that month William Marwood adjusted the noose around her neck.

In 1883 Marwood, now sixty-three years old, was taken ill at his home in Horncastle, Lincolnshire. Suffering from inflammation of the lungs, complicated by jaundice, there was little hope for him, and on 4 September he passed away. He was buried in Trinity churchyard, in Horncastle, and his demise was lamented by newspapers throughout the country, for he had brought some mercy to his victims, some respectability to his calling.

As the nineteenth century progressed, the categories of crimes carrying the death penalty were drastically reduced, from over 200 in 1826 to only four in 1861, these being murder, treason, piracy with violence, and arson in royal vessels, dockyards and arsenals. The number of hangings declined accordingly, from ninety-eight in 1819–21, to as few as five in 1843–5, in the London and Middlesex area. And as these took place out of sight behind prison walls, the public found more innocuous entertainment elsewhere, in the music halls and theatres, newspapers and magazines.

Even the ghoulish vocabulary which had grown up around the hanging scene faded from the public's memory. Only the veteran scaffold devotees could recall when a hanging day was known as wryneck day (awry, with neck on one side), when Fridays were called hangman's day because that was when the event took place, although later the law decreed that the sun should not set a second time on a convicted murderer, unless a Sunday intervened. So judges tried offenders on a Friday, the hanging taking place at 8 a.m. on the Monday.

Going to Tyburn was 'going to Scrag'em Fair' or 'Paddington Fair', Tyburn being in the parish of Paddington. There, one would see the gallows, the triangular ones being the 'three legged mare'. Other jocular names for the fearsome structure were the 'Sheriff's picture frame' and because of its obvious resemblance, the 'Gregorian tree' (after Gregory Brandon, the hangman) and the 'deadly never-green', the victims hanging on its branches being 'gallows apples' or 'Jack Ketch's Pippins'.

The victim was transported by cart, the 'gaoler's coach', and the hangman himself was known as a topping cove, a topping fellow, a crapping cull (from fifteenth-century Old Dutch *crappen*, to break or snap), a scragboy, and Lord of the Manor of Tyburn. In Scotland his nicknames were the doomster, the dempster or the staffman.

Around the felon's neck went the noose, the 'Tyburn collar' or 'Tyburn tippet', the 'anodyne necklace' (anodyne meaning relief from pain), the hempen casement, hempen habeas, the neckweed (hemp again), the hempen cravat and the hempen snare. His ailment was hempen fever and his wife later known as a hempen widow.

After the knot had been positioned at the 'haltering place' beneath the left ear, the felon was blindfolded with 'Paddington spectacles'. The trapdoor was then released, this being 'the fall of the leaf' and the victim then 'danced the Newgate hornpipe', the 'Paddington frisk' or more elaborately, 'danced at the Sheriff's Ball and lolled his tongue out at the company'.

Other apt descriptions were; to go to rest in a horse's nightcap (halter), to be stabbed by a Bridport dagger (a Dorset town where hempen rope was manufactured) and, somewhat vulgarly, to 'have a wry mouth and a pisson pair of breeches'. Morbid detail was evidenced in the phrase 'to be scragged, ottomised and then grin in a glass case' (to be hanged, dissected, i.e. anatomized, and one's skeleton then exhibited at Surgeons' Hall). The more erudite spectator preferred the phrase 'Sus. per Coll.', the words 'suspensus per collum' (hung by the neck) being entered in the gaol book.

The last words spoken by some of the victims in the 'good old days' were also treasured by those who appreciated such literary gems. Long remembered were the immortal words uttered by wife-murderer William Borwick who, while standing on York's scaffold, commented that he hoped the rope was strong enough because if it broke he'd fall to the ground and be crippled for life! And William Palmer, the Rugeley poisoner, when escorted on to the drop, turned to the hangman and said 'Are you sure it's safe?' Men of wit, if not of morality.

By the end of the nineteenth century it could be said that the great days of English hanging were over. Marwood's humane methods were adopted and improved on by later hangmen, notably by the dedicated and efficient dynasty of the Pierrepoints in the early twentieth century. Hangings were few in number, and took place unseen, and with hangmen thus becoming impersonal government officials, general interest waned.

Exploits of this century's executioners have been well chronicled, some by the hangmen themselves, who related highlights of their careers, the dispatching of notorious murderers and war criminals. Many of these accounts are of but academic interest, the proceedings revealing the clinical details of the executions which, while being tributes to the skill and expertise of the men in charge, lack the human drama, the frenzied atmosphere of the times when hangings were a public spectacle.

Ironically it was not until the annual number of hangings had dwindled to single figures that, in 1885, the Home Office finally got around to designing a standard pattern for scaffolds, one which would reduce mechanical failure of the apparatus to a minimum. For the technically minded, it consisted of a heavy cross-beam high in the walls of the execution chamber, into which hooks were fixed for the attachment of the ropes.

Set in the floor beneath the beam were two large trapdoors of three-inch oak, hinged to the side walls of the pit below. The three hinges of trap A were elongated beyond its width, trap B thereby resting on them when in the closed position. The ends of the extended hinge arms rested on an iron drawbar one and a quarter inches thick which ran longitudinally beneath trap B, the bar having three slots corresponding to, but not aligned with, the hinge ends.

The operation of the drop lever caused the drawbar to slide rapidly along until the hinge ends, lining up with the bar's slots, dropped through them. The sheer weight of the heavy trapdoors, plus that of the victim, caused the doors to swing down, instantly launching the victim into the brick-lined pit below, until the rope jerked taut.

To prevent the doors bouncing back on impact with the pit walls, spring catches held and retained them vertically. For 'reloading', trap B was first raised and held vertically. Trap A was then lifted, to be positioned with the ends of its hinge arms resting on the drawbar. Trap B was then lowered ninety degrees, to be supported by the now horizontally extended hinge arms, and all was then ready for the next execution.

In order that justice could be administered unimpeded, provision had to be made for victims who fainted on the scaffold or were otherwise disabled. So a stretcher was available, to which an unconscious prisoner could be strapped, and it is assumed that both victim and stretcher would fall together, the extra weight having been taken into consideration. Warders, standing on planks, invariably flanked the prisoners on the drop, and so would support a one-legged or similarly handicapped person.

Among the unique accessories exhibited in Lancaster Castle is the hanging chair, a child's high chair fitted with restraining straps and castor wheels. It was used at the execution of 21-year-old Jane Scott who, in 1828, was the last woman to be publicly hanged there. She was sentenced to death for having murdered her mother by administering rat poison and by the time of her execution, Jane had become so emaciated that, unable to walk to the gallows, she was wheeled there in the specially adapted high chair. On the drop the noose was placed around her neck, the chair was withdrawn, and Jane Scott paid the price for her crime.

But that was not the end of the story. By kind permission of the *Lancashire Evening Post* I am able to relate the subsequent gruesome disposal of poor Jane's bones. Her cadaver was purchased by Dr Thomas Monk of the nearby town of Preston, who died some sixty years later, and the wired-up skeleton was acquired by a herbalist, Mr Livesey. After some initial repugnance, 'Old Jane' became one of the family, her appearance being improved by the application of whitewash, though somewhat marred by a pink spot on her skull where rain had dripped from a leaky roof.

The Livesey grandchildren accepted her as an unprotesting and highly flexible playmate, occasionally using her forearms as drumsticks. However, during a burglary at the herbal shop, the skull was stolen, and when eventually the family moved house, some bones were buried in the front garden, the rest being handed in as museum items.

Similar pieces of equipment to the hanging chair are disposed of whenever a prison is closed down. When in 1903 Newgate Prison was demolished, some of the actual cells which housed notorious criminals were bought by Madame Tussaud's, the Waxworks owners also paying

£100 for the old prison bell which was tolled when executions took place.

The equipment from the prison's execution shed was sold elsewhere for £5 15s, but its old-style triple scaffold was transferred to Pentonville Prison in London where it was subsequently modified. Its operating equipment consisted of two doors, each eight feet long by two and a half feet wide, which were released when bolts set in the side walls were withdrawn by the drop lever. From the two cross-beams overhead, hung chains, adjustable in length, to which the ropes would be attached.

This scaffold gave many years of service but was phased out of use following the last death sentences in 1964. However, one operational scaffold still survives, Wandsworth Prison having the facilities with which to execute those found guilty of piracy with violence, treason, and other mutinous offences enacted under the Armed Forces Act 1971, these crimes still nominally carrying the death penalty. The equipment is tested every six months, the machinery being oiled and the trapdoors operated to ensure their efficient functioning.

Other neighbouring countries hanged their criminals, of course. They had their gallows, their scaffolds and their idiosyncratic executioners. One in particular operated in the Irish town of Roscommon early in the last century, and anyone under the impression that callousness is the sole prerogative of the male sex would be sadly mistaken, for the executioner was a woman known as Lady Betty, a 'Lady of the Scaffold', no less!

This Jill O'Ketch of the Connaught circuit was described in the *Dublin University Magazine* of January 1850 as a middle-aged, stout-made, swarthy-complexioned but by no means forbidding-looking woman, well educated though possessing a violent temper.

When younger, she had treated her son so harshly that he left home and enlisted in the army. After service in foreign parts, he returned to Ireland and, now much changed in appearance and curious to see whether his mother had mellowed at all, he adopted another identity when asking her for a few nights' lodgings. To be concise, she hadn't, and he shouldn't have done, for while he was asleep, his mother murdered him for his savings.

She was condemned to death, together with some cattle thieves and sheep stealers, but no hangman was available. As the magazine with heavy sarcasm reported:

> time was pressing and the sheriff and deputy, being men of refinement, education, humanity and sensibility, who could not be expected to fulfil the office which they had undertaken, and for which one of them at least was paid, this wretched woman, being the only one who could be found to perform this office, consented.

Lady Betty adopted her new career with relish. Not for her a mask and disguise, for such would have been quite superfluous, and she hanged and flogged with enthusiasm all those delivered into her capable hands.

The scaffolds in the old Irish towns were designed to give an uninterrupted view to the maximum number of spectators, the Roscommon one being an excellent example. The third storey of the town gaol was pierced by a doorway over which projected a beam. Level with this entrance, or rather exit, was a hinged platform with a sliding bolt holding it horizontal until the noose had been positioned and prayers recited. When the bolt was withdrawn, the platform would drop against the prison wall with a crash that echoed around the town, leaving the felon suspended from the beam.

After the execution Lady Betty would accompany the corpse in a cart to the market square where two tall poles had been erected. With the assistance of the gaolers she would hoist the body high, its arms widely secured to the poles, gibbet fashion, as a deterrent to all.

Returning to her home she would then, according to the aforementioned magazine, draw a charcoal portrait of her victim on the wall of her home, using a burnt stick. And so fearsome was her reputation that children of the neighbourhood quickly made up their minds to stop misbehaving and go off to sleep, upon being threatened by their irate parents: 'huggath a' Pooka', here comes Lady Betty!

The Irish and English scaffolds contrasted markedly with those of France, although generally all were sited for maximum spectator enjoyment. Until the Revolution and its single method of execution France, like England, dispatched its upper class offenders by means of decapitation and eliminated many common criminals by hanging.

Most towns in France had their gallows, two or more stone pillars surmounted by timber cross-beams from which the victims were suspended. As befitted the capital city, Paris boasted the finest, this being situated on a hill nearby. On a raised platform about ten yards wide and fifteen yards long, ten stone pillars had been erected around the perimeter, each thirty feet high. These were joined at the top by cross-beams, with hanging chains to which the ropes would eventually be tied.

As related in Lacroix's *Manners, Customs and Costumes of the Middle Ages*, the prisoner was taken by cart, seated facing backwards, to the gallows. There the executioner placed two nooses around the felon's neck, plus a third rope called a 'jet'. Ascending the ladder backwards, he pulled the victim up with him until he was able to secure the noosed ropes to the chains. With a quick jerk of the 'jet' the hangman pulled the felon off the ladder and, in much the same way as the more ruthless English executioners, he assisted in his victim's demise by adding his own weight to that of the felon. Because of the height of the gallows beam from the ground however, pulling the victim's legs, English-fashion, was not possible, but the French executioner achieved the same result by standing on the bound wrists of the victim, stirrup-style, and jerking downwards until life was extinct.

Across the border in Germany, the penalties were much the same, beheading for the upper-class criminal, the disgrace of hanging for the plebeian felon. Originally the rope was made of withies, this material later being replaced by hemp.

Youthfulness was no excuse when the scaffold beckoned. In 1584 five young lads, having been previously whipped and placed in the stocks for stealing, were hanged at Nuremberg, despite their being only thirteen, fifteen, sixteen, seventeen and twenty-two years old. Women too suffered the same fate unless granted the privilege of the sword. In 1583 three prostitutes were pilloried and whipped out of town. Later they were caught breaking into houses and stealing valuables, so for their offences one had her ears cut off, and she and a companion were hanged.

German executioners were just as prone as other nationalities to make mistakes on the scaffold, one instance being in 1620 when a new hangman, Bernard Schlegel, had beginner's nerves on the scaffold. After his victim had been turned off the ladder, probably by the assistant hangman, Schlegel remained astride the cross-beam. Whether, being thus marooned without the ladder, he panicked, will never be known, but in order to end the ordeal he pulled the victim's hair in desperation, then pressed down on the man's head in an attempt to speed the victim's death.

The crowd, incensed by these amateurish actions, showed their disapproval in the time-honoured way by storming the scaffold, and Schlegel, thanks to his assistant's alacrity in replacing the ladder, was fortunate to escape with his life.

Regrettably, executions by the rope continued well into the twentieth century in Great Britain and on the Continent. Hundreds of prisoners were hanged in German concentration camps in the Second World War, the victims having to stand on the retractable seats of chairs, the ropes being secured to hooks on the wall above them. The inevitable short drop resulted in strangulation, and many of those responsible received their just deserts, albeit with a more merciful long drop, after the Nuremberg War Trials.

Behind English prison walls judicial hangings conti-nued until capital punishment was abolished in 1965. The last two men to be executed were Peter Anthony Allen and Gwynne Owen Evans, convicted of murdering John West with a cosh and a knife, in Seaton, Northumberland. Tried and sentenced to death, they were duly hanged at 8 a.m.

on 13 August 1964, Allen at Walton Gaol, Liverpool, Evans at Strangeways Prison, Manchester.

5   Warriors of the Wheel

On 5 November each year people celebrate Bonfire Night, lighting fireworks to commemorate the failure of the Gunpowder Plot of 1605, and recalling the fate of the Plotters, many of whom were hanged, drawn and quartered. But a punishment just as barbaric as that is remembered in the harmless little firework, the Catherine Wheel.

The Catherine of the title was Saint Catherine, who lived in Alexandria, Egypt, in the fourth century. At that time the Romans ruled the country and Catherine, an intelligent young woman, protested vehemently against the harsh treatment to which the Christians were being subjected.

Legend has it that on the orders of Emperor Maxentius, fifty philosophers attempted to argue the religious facts with her. Not only did they fail to make their point, but they themselves were converted by her, a hollow victory because the Emperor promptly had the wise men put to death.

Changing his strategy, Maxentius next endeavoured to quell Catherine's protests by offering her a consort's crown, but when she indignantly refused it, he had her beaten and thrown into prison. There, unbeknown to the Emperor, she was visited by the Emperor's wife, whereupon Catherine proceeded to convert her to Christianity as well.

This defiance signed Catherine's death warrant, Maxentius sentencing her to death on a spiked wheel. This device, in contrast to the type used later on the Continent for executions, was a large vertical wheel with spikes protruding from each rim, as if extensions of the spokes. Catherine was strapped to the circumference of the wheel, between the spikes, and her torturers then began to propel the wheel over other spikes set upright in the ground.

But divine providence interceded, for the wheel broke, the spikes flying off and injuring many bystanders. Driven beyond endurance, the Emperor sentenced her to be beheaded, whereupon, it is alleged, milk rather than blood flowed from her corpse.

Saint Catherine, understandably, is the patron saint of wheelwrights and philosophers among others, and in England sixty-two churches are dedicated to her and 170 medieval steeple bells bear her name.

A hospital was also named after her. It was founded in 1148 by Queen Matilda, wife of King Stephen, and was situated by the River Thames, immediately east of the Tower of London. Queens of England were patronesses, and its priests and staff cared for the sick, travellers, women and children. The inmates of the hospital wore straight coats decorated with the wheel of the saint, and were allowed to go into the City but had to return before the curfew sounded.

Much of the hospital grounds was acquired by later monarchs in order to increase the Tower's defences, and in 1825 the City of London took over all the buildings and surrounding streets, their demolition allowing huge docks to be built there capable of receiving more than 200 ships, the wharfs surrounded by cavernous warehouses for the storage of riches from the East, cotton, wines, silks and rich spices.

In turn the docks themselves became redundant and within the last twenty years a splendid yacht marina and shopping centre have been developed there, and the discerning visitor will find plaques set in the walls, engraved with a wheel and the name of St Katherine's Dock.

Far from being pleasant decoration however, the wheel as used for punishment on the Continent was an appallingly cruel device. Never adopted in Britain, it was introduced into France from Germany about 1534 during the reign of Francis I, and was generally reserved for the punishment of robbers and thieves, although other criminals were certainly eligible.

The French device consisted of a large wheel mounted horizontally on a short post. On the wheel were secured two lengths of wood in the shape of a St Andrew's cross to which the spread-eagled victim was tied. The cross-pieces were hollowed out beneath arms, thighs and shins, so that only the joints of the limbs were supported.

The executioner, using an iron bar three feet long and two inches square, would strike the limb over each hollow, thereby shattering each arm and leg in two places. After the requisite eight blows, the victim received the *coup de grâce*, further blows to the chest bringing death. On very rare occasions the *retentum* could be administered, a merciful strangulation with a cord, after a certain number of blows had been delivered.

Alexandre Dumas described in one of his books the punishment meted out to a Protestant, Boeton. The equipment differed from that detailed above, in that the St Andrew's cross was on a low platform. Following the breaking of his limbs, his mutilated body was lifted up and, like a pitiful ragdoll, was placed over a horizontally mounted wheel so that the crowd could witness his dying moments.

One well-documented and horrific case was the 'breaking on the wheel' of two French noblemen, Antoine-Joseph, Count de Horn, a cousin of the Regent, and his friend the Chevalier de Milhe, in March 1720. In need of money to finance their extravagant way of life, they murdered a Jew in a tavern and stole 100,000 livres from him.

Despite their aristocratic connections they were sentenced to death, the Regent rejecting the many petitions raised on behalf of de Horn; some even pleaded that his family had a history of insanity.

The executioner was Charles Sanson, grandfather of the renowned Charles-Henri. Charles had been Lord of the Scaffold since 1699, contemporaries describing him as a gentle and even-tempered man. In 1707 he had married Marthe Dubut, and because of the closely knit families of headsmen, their guest list included his stepmother (widow of Charles Sanson I and sister to the bride), Nicholas Le Marshand (executioner of Nantes, cousin of the bride) and his wife, and also Marguerite Jouanne, widow of one executioner and later married to another.

Charles Sanson II had prospered in his career, and lived in style and luxury in a large mansion in Paris. Even discounting his loyalty and dedication to his job, he had no need to consider the bribes offered him to allow de Horn to escape. And when offered rather more personal favours by the ravishing Marquise de Parabère, the Regent's mistress, he still refused to help, for rumours abounded that the Regent, having discovered that the Marquise had been having an affair with the doomed 22-year-old Count, saw this as an excellent opportunity to dispose of his rival.

When Sanson collected his two victims, they had already been tortured in order to discover the names of any other accomplices, and had to be helped into the tumbril. On the scaffold de Horn and de Milhe were each strapped to a wheel but Sanson, without authority though perhaps through mercy, or fear of the Count's influential relatives, surreptitiously passed a cord around de Horn's neck and tightened it before the last crushing blow was delivered by his assistant. The ghastly charade was continued until the dead man's limbs had been duly shattered.

The Count's accomplice, de Milhe, was not so fortunate. Lacking powerful allies at Court, he suffered the full penalty, until Sanson ordered the *coup de grâce* and his assistant aimed the final blow to the victim's chest.

Of the scores of victims sentenced to be broken on the wheel, probably the most unjustly condemned was a young man, Jean Louschart. His decidedly left-wing views clashed with those of his father Mathurin, a blacksmith, who was an ardent royalist. The dispute eventually came to a head over Hélène, the daughter of their housekeeper. The two youngsters fell in love, a match strongly opposed by Hélène's mother, who saw better prospects for herself and her daughter if Hélène could be persuaded to marry Mathurin, the father. A furious row ensued, the older man being so incensed by his son's attitude that, picking up one of his hammers, he tried to strike Jean. Being younger and fitter, Jean wrested the implement from him, strode to the door and threw the hammer over his shoulder, back into the room. Tragically it struck his father, killing him instantly.

Jean, distraught with grief and remorse, was put on trial. Resigned to die, he accepted the court's sentence, that he be broken on the wheel.

The scaffold was erected in the place St Louis in Versailles, and there Jean Louschart was taken, to face Charles-Henri Sanson, the executioner. The inevitable crowd had gathered, but this was a crowd with a difference. Many of them were revolutionary friends of Jean, others of similar anti-royalist sympathies, sentiments that were to grow to explosive proportions only a few months later.

Accordingly, before Sanson and his assistants could bind Louschart on to the wheel, the crowd rushed the scaffold and freed the condemned man from his captors. The assistants fled in terror and from a safe distance Sanson watched as the mob smashed the wheel and St Andrew's cross, demolished the scaffold, and threw the debris on to the fire which had been kindled to burn the victim's body after mutilation.

Rarely has an intended execution had such a happy ending. On hearing the details, King Louis XVI pardoned Jean Louschart and, later that year, 1788, the penalty of being broken on the wheel was abolished. History does not record, unfortunately, whether Jean married Hélène!

In the neighbouring country of Germany the wheel had been in use for many centuries, its design differing slightly from its French counterpart. The German wheel was supported on a tripod, the nave, at the wheel's hub, resting on a short stub so that the wheel could be turned easily. No St Andrew's cross was used, and tripods varied in height so that blows could be delivered from either above or below.

Breaking on the German wheel was a punishment reserved mainly for murderers and, far more drastic than French punishment, the regulation number of strokes with the sharp-edged bar was forty, the last one being directed at the chest or the nape of the neck.

In the sixteenth and seventeenth centuries many criminals were subjected to that agonizing death. On 2 January 1588 two murderers, George Hornlein and Jobst Knau, embarked on a series of brutal crimes which were to end on the scaffold. Hornlein had previously stabbed a man to death and stolen his money; he and Knau then shot and robbed another man. Later, while living with a woman who had given birth to a child, one of them cut off its hand, probably to use as a Hand of Glory. He then strangled the infant and buried it in the garden.

For those and other crimes the two felons were taken by tumbril to the Nuremberg scaffold. Master Franz Schmidt, Warrior of the Wheel, skilled not only with the sword and rope, had prepared another little refinement for his clients. As ordered by the court, 'both their arms were twice nipped with red-hot tongs and their right arms and legs were broken. Lastly, they were executed on the wheel.'

Hans Kolben was another notorious criminal in the Nuremberg area. Captured after stabbing his wife and later an innocent wayfarer, he was imprisoned in Königshofen Tower. Being a man of resource however, he loosened some stones in his cell, using a bone, and got clean away, to continue his life of violence. One of his victims who tried to resist was struck by an axe wielded by Kolben, and subsequently died.

The murderer managed to elude the police and, changing his criminal activities, took to counterfeiting currency. Success going to his head, he started to manufacture coins on such a large scale that eventually he was arrested and held in a tower in Klein Amburg. Again he escaped, this time using a rope, but fell heavily, injuring himself. Recaptured, he soon found that the Nuremberg gaol was more than a match for him. In an attempt to thwart justice, he bit a large piece of flesh out of his arm, hoping that he might bleed to death. But to no avail, for on 11 July 1598 he was taken to the scaffold.

Spurning the attention of the priest, he told the good man to be quiet; he had, he said, heard it all before, and didn't want to hear it again because it made his head ache. Franz Schmidt wasted little time in securing him to the wheel. All four limbs were broken with the iron bar and after his execution by further heavy blows, his body was burnt to ashes.

That manner of death would seem to be agonizing enough by itself, yet again and again, executioners had to add that little extra, the nip with the red-hot tongs, before getting down to the really serious business on the wheel. As Michael Gemperlein found out on 5 March 1612, after a criminal career as a highwayman, during which he had murdered four men and two women, and robbed many more. His body was torn four times with the red-hot tongs before being subjected to the ultimate punishment.

There is little doubt, however, that for some criminals even the wheel was not punishment enough. In 1574 Kloss Renckhart of Fehlsdorf shot his companion and also a miller's man who had helped him to attack and plunder a mill by night. At another mill, the Fox mill, he and a confederate shot the miller dead, injured the miller's wife and maid, then made them fry some eggs in fat. Kloss then put the eggs on the dead miller's body and forced the wife to join in the meal. Kicking the corpse, Renckhart exclaimed: 'Well, miller, how do you like this morsel?' On being taken from the mill wheel to Schmidt's wheel, the brutal murderer endured the pulverizing blows delivered by the executioner, before succumbing to the final blow to his chest.

Not all executions were applauded by the crowd, of course. On one occasion, when a gypsy was to receive his just deserts, the wheel was decorated with flowers placed there by the condemned man's sweetheart.

Throughout his career as a Lord of the Scaffold and Warrior of the Wheel, Schmidt was more or less successful in maintaining his impartiality when acting as a servant of the State. Yet his emotions must have been sorely strained when, in 1585, he had to execute his own brother-in-law. *En route* to the scaffold on Nuremberg's Rabenstein, he administered only two tweaks with the hot tongs, the rest having been remitted by the court as a special favour.

On the scaffold the condemned man was allowed to embrace his daughter before being dispatched by Franz, receiving thirty-one strokes of the bar before expiring.

One cannot really visualize a more brutal way of administering – or receiving – a death sentence, and thankfully this particular punishment disappeared from the judicial history of those countries in the early nineteenth century.

6   Fellowship of the Firing Squad

Every day hundreds of tourists visiting the Tower of London approach the Chapel Royal of St Peter ad Vincula with the guided tours conducted by the yeoman warders. As they do so they step on a large paving stone, one which differs from its fellow stones by being black. It has no distinguishing marks, no inscriptions, yet it bears mute witness to one of the saddest episodes in the history of the British Army.

Early in the morning of 18 July 1743, Londoners heard gunfire coming from the Tower of London. Doubtless they attributed it to musket practice within the walls. Little did they realize that it was the sound of British soldiers killing other British soldiers in that historic castle, the culmination of an event which started months earlier in Scotland.

There, 800 men of Lord Sempill's Regiment (later to become the Black Watch) were instructed to march to London, to be inspected by King George II. These 'gentlemen Highlanders', sons of wealthy landowners and farmers, arrived in the capital on 30 April, only to find that the King had gone to Hanover. Worse was to follow, for rumours spread that, far from returning home, they had been lured south to be shipped to the West Indies on indefinite duty.

Their morale was already low, their pay in arrears, their living conditions in camp at Finchley deplorable. Ripe for desertion, 109 of them led by Corporal Samuel McPherson set off at 1 a.m. on 18 May, and headed north back towards Scotland, not as a mutinous rabble but as a well-disciplined body of men.

When the alarm was raised, three companies of dragoons were sent in pursuit. Civilian co-operation was also encouraged by the reward offered, forty shillings bonus for each man captured. And at Lady Wood, near Brigstock in Northamptonshire, the deserters were intercepted by the dragoons, to whom they surrendered without resistance. Reduced by sickness to 101 in number, they were escorted under heavy guard to London and taken to the Tower.

There the men were well treated and well fed. 'They were allowed a pd. and a half of bread, half a pd. of good chees and a Pynt of Oatmeal per day, which I provided for them, and received 4d. per day each man,' reported Lt General Adam Williamson, Lieutenant of the Tower.

On 8 June the inevitable courts martial commenced in the Lieutenant's lodgings (now the Queen's House), twenty men a day being tried. Showing some clemency, the court found only three guilty, the ringleaders Samuel McPherson, his cousin Malcolm McPherson, and Farquar Shaw. Far from being young hot-heads, they were in their thirties, of good families and in fact had tried to dissuade their comrades from taking their rash actions. Despite their petitions for mercy, the three men were sentenced to death by firing squad.

At 6 a.m. on 18 July 1743, all the deserters with the exception of the condemned men were paraded on Tower Green, the open space where, centuries before, three queens of England had cruelly died; where today's tourists picnic in the sunshine. The Highlanders were formed up into a large semi-circle facing the Chapel Royal, whilst spaced out behind them, to control any revolt, were 300 men of the 3rd Regiment of Guards – ironically, now the Scots Guards.

The wall of the Chapel facing Tower Green now has five windows, but in the eighteenth century there were only four, the right-hand, easterly end of the wall being solid and unbroken. On that fateful morning two planks lay on the rough ground in front of the wall, and the three condemned men, wearing shrouds under their clothes, knelt on one plank. Two ministers, Campbell and Paterson, faced them, kneeling on the other plank.

After nine minutes of prayer, in which all the Highlanders knelt and joined, the ministers moved away and the three men were ordered to pull their caps down over their eyes. As described by General Williamson, who was present:

> All this while, they saw not the men appointed by lot to shoot them, which made Samuel McPherson, the bravest of them, say, what, are we not to be shott, where are the men who are to shoot us? To this was answered, if you'll draw your caps over your faces you'll soon be dispatched.

What the condemned men were mercifully unaware of, was that eighteen men, twelve for the firing squad, six in reserve, had previously been stationed round the east side of the Chapel (where now the Jewel House queue winds its circuitous way), the men being kept out of sight so as not to shock the prisoners.

At a given signal, wrote General Williamson:

> they now advanced on Tiptoe round the corner of the Chapple and with the least noise possible, their Muskets already being cocked for fear of the Click disturbing the Prisoners, Sergeant Major Ellison (who deserves a greatest Commendation for taking this Precaution) waved a handkerchief as a Signal to present, and after a very short Pause, as they aimed four to a man, waved it a second time as a Signal 'to Fire'. All three men fell instantly backwards as dead, but Shaw, being observed to move his hand, one of the six Reserve advanced and shot him through the head, as did another, to shoot Samuel McPherson through the ear.

This tragic scene, made more heart-rending because it involved Scot killing Scot, soldier killing soldier, rather than an impersonal executioner eliminating common criminals, left no spectator unmoved. The officers on duty, even the hardened Scots Guards surrounding the deserters, were visibly overcome, many of them in tears.

The bodies were stripped to their shrouds and gently placed in the waiting coffins, which were then buried near the Chapel door, the spot marked only by the black flagstone. Whether guilty of a serious military crime or not, they rest in not unworthy company, for within yards of their last resting place lie the remains of Queen Anne Boleyn, Queen Catherine Howard, Lady Jane Grey and the others who met their deaths within the Tower.

The remainder of the grief-stricken deserters were duly punished. Marched to Gravesend, thirty were sent to Gibraltar, twenty each to Minorca and the Leeward Isles and the remaining twenty-eight to Jamaica. From these postings, uncivilized and disease-ridden in those days, few if any returned.

The only other deaths by firing squad in the Tower of London were however of a very different nature, devoid of sentiment, lacking in sympathy. For when world wars raged and enemy spies were caught, tried and sentenced, there could be only one result – the death penalty.

During the First World War, eleven spies died facing the firing squads in the Tower, the first being Carl Hans Lody on 6 November 1914. He was followed by Breekouw and Müller in June of the next year, then Roos and Janssen in July. Roggin and Melin were shot in September, Buschmann and Ries in October 1915. In December Meyer was executed and then Hurwitz in April 1916. All were buried in the East London Cemetery, Plaistow, Lody's grave having a black marble headstone, the names of the others being engraved on a nearby memorial stone slab.

They were all executed in the small rifle range, a hut situated between the inner and outer walls of the Tower, less than twenty yards from the dwelling occupied by the author and his wife when resident there. The range, demolished in 1969, stood adjacent to the Martin Tower, once the prison of such notables as the Duke of Northumberland and later Ambrose Rookwood, a Gunpowder Plotter. In due course it became the Jewel House, scene of Colonel Blood's attempted robbery of the Regalia in 1671, and more recently it housed yeoman warders and their families.

The range was originally roofless and it has been reported that not only did some Tower residents watch the executions from the battlements of the inner wall, but also the young daughter of the Martin Tower family, who had an excellent vantage point from her bedroom window! Inevitably this was discovered (a result of nightmares?) and an irate father re-organized the sleeping arrangements!

After the First World War the range, by then roofed, continued to be used for small-arms practice. Only once more did its walls echo to the squad's deafening salvo of shots, that taking place at 7.12 a.m. on 15 August 1941 when Josef Jakobs suffered the supreme penalty.

Jakobs, a Feldwebel (sergeant) of the German Army seconded to the Meteorological Branch, had been parachuted into England on 31 January 1941, his forty-third birthday, incidentally. Information on the weather was vital to the German Air Force in order to plan their bombing raids. The Royal Air Force was more fortunate in that respect, the weather over the British Isles usually moving on into Europe and so being taken into consideration when operations against Continental targets were being planned.

Josef Jakobs landed in a potato field in North Stifford, Essex, falling heavily and breaking his ankle. Unable to walk, or even to bury his tell-tale parachute, he was found by a farm worker, and a local army unit took him into custody.

When he was captured he was found to be wearing a parachutist's helmet and flying suit, beneath which was a grey pin-striped suit and, of all things, spats. To complete his English gentleman's attire, he also carried a brown bowler hat, though the absence of an umbrella would have probably led to immediate penetration of his disguise!

Near to his half-buried parachute lay a suitcase containing a loaded revolver, a false identity card, ration cards, and a quantity of food which included a large German sausage. There was also £500 in one-pound notes, and a five-valve radio transmitter.

In the face of such damning evidence Jakobs had little defence against the charge of being a spy. He faced a general court martial on 4 August and, despite his plea of being a meteorologist rather than a combat soldier, he was found guilty and sentenced to be shot by firing squad, the only spy to be so executed in the Second World War. Other spies, namely Timmerman, Vanhove, Walberg, Meier, Kieboom, Drueke, Waelt, Richter, Winters, Dronkers and Nevermans, being civilians, were hanged, some at Pentonville, the others at Wandsworth Prison.

Jakobs was held in the Waterloo Block of the Tower of London until the fateful day, 15 August, when he was taken under armed guard to the rifle range. The sombre occasion was made even more macabre by one of the Tower ravens, those mythical harbingers of death, which had ventured from its customary territory around Tower Green. It now stood croaking at the armed party's approach, and although the officer in charge tried to drive the bird away, the yeoman warders present pointed out the futility of the attempt, and the raven remained nearby, not returning to its companions until after the execution.

Upon entering the range Jakobs, because of his injured ankle, was permitted to sit in a chair. A circular piece of white lint was pinned over his heart as an aiming point and the firing squad, of the Scots Guards, opened fire. Five bullets pierced the lint, killing the spy instantly.

The body was taken for a post-mortem examination to the mortuary, a gloomy little room in the outer wall of the moat, immediately beneath the approach road to Tower Bridge. Following the autopsy, the body was buried in St Mary's Roman Catholic Cemetery at Kensal Green, London.

The chair, an ordinary brown Windsor type, is still in the Tower, though not on view to the public. When inspected by the author, it was seen to have the back supporting rails shot away, evidence of the hail of bullets fired on that fateful day.

Enough about the victims – what about the members of a firing squad? To aim to kill in battle poses no problems, but to kill in cold blood, as part of a firing squad rather than as an assassin or terrorist, can only be accomplished by members of the military machine, accepting unquestioningly the rules laid down. When one acts in accordance with legitimate orders, one does not have to think, just obey.

In that respect all national armies are the same, the following American procedure during the Second World War being a good example of who does what, when and how. Never why!

The officer in charge has to instruct the escort and firing squad in their duties, the latter party consisting of twelve men and a sergeant. A chaplain, a medical officer and an ambulance are to be in attendance, and a firm wooden post is to be erected at the execution site, fitted with rings to secure the prisoner in an upright position.

The officer in charge has to provide a black hood as a blindfold, and a four-inch circular white target. He will supervise the loading of twelve rifles, not less than one nor more than four of which will be loaded with blank ammunition, a merciful panacea for the troubled conscience, and he will ensure that the rifles are placed randomly in the rack.

A military band is deemed necessary and is to form up facing the scene of execution. Behind the band will be paraded witnessing troops, to form three sides of a rectangle. Meanwhile the members of the firing squad will each select a rifle from the rack and take up position fifteen paces from, and facing the post.

The prisoner, his arms bound behind his back, will be marched from his prison, escorted by twelve soldiers armed with rifles, under the command of a sergeant with a pistol. As they approach, the band will play the 'Dead March' (even executions have to have their signature tunes, it seems), and will move to the flank of the rectangle, to allow the main guard to form a line five paces behind the firing squad, facing the site of the execution.

The officer in charge, now facing the prisoner, will read out the charge, the court's findings and the sentence, and will then ask the chaplain to approach, in order to receive any last statements from the condemned man.

The sergeant of the firing squad then secures the prisoner to the post and places the hood over his head, the medical officer next attaching the target disc over the man's heart. The chaplain and medical officer then move clear, as does the escort.

The officer in charge positions himself five paces to the right of, and five paces to the front of the firing squad.

As with all well-defined military regulations, every possible contingency is catered for. So in the event of the execution taking place in a sensitive area, perhaps near civilian dwellings, or where the noise of battle would drown all other sounds, the execution commands would be given manually. Doubtless the band would be similarly dispensed with, to the relief of all present!

In such an eventuality the firing squad would come to the 'Ready' position and unlock rifles (safety catches 'off'), on seeing the officer raise his right arm vertically, palm forward, fingers extended and together. Upon the lowering of his arm to the horizontal position in front of him, the squad would aim their weapons. And when he dropped his arm to his side and ordered 'Fire!', the squad would pull the triggers.

When oral commands were the order of the day, the three commands Ready, Aim, and Fire would be used.

The officer and medical officer will then inspect the prisoner. If a *coup de grâce* is necessary, it will be administered by the sergeant of the firing squad, who will fire his pistol twelve inches from the prisoner's skull, just above the ear. Exceptionally, an extra file of six men may administer the *coup de grâce*, should the sergeant be unable to, for any reason, and will open fire while standing in front of the firing squad.

After the medical officer has confirmed the prisoner's death, the rifles will be replaced randomly in the rack, no member thereby knowing whether he has fired a live round or not, and the squad will then dismiss.

The witnessing troops are marched past the body, while the band plays 'a lively air' (!), and will return to their barracks. The detailed burial party will then convey the body to the morgue for subsequent burial.

Not all wartime firing squads acted in accordance with the Geneva Convention, however. As disclosed at the Nuremberg War Trials, over a hundred and fifty French and Italian officers, and thousands of Russian prisoners of war, were executed by German firing squads at Dachau concentration camp. Some of the victims were shot with .98 calibre rifles at a range of thirty yards. Others, stripped, had to kneel with their backs to the SS firing squads who then shot them in the back of the neck, using pistols.

Tragically, four British women of the Special Operations Executive (SOE), who had been parachuted into France to assist the Resistance, were also shot at Dachau. In 1944 they were shot in the back of the neck, whilst holding hands with each other, their bodies afterwards being cremated.

A hundred and fifty years earlier, French civilian firing squads were busy in the Vendée region, eliminating the 'enemies' of the Revolution, for not even the number of guillotines provided could cope with the influx of victims. No aristocrats these, but peasants threatened by the religious intolerance of the revolutionary authorities in Paris. In Rennes a company of children was recruited from the more affluent middle class. This group was called 'The Hope of our Country' and they were employed to shoot those caught and condemned by the militia.

The executions took place in the Saint Etienne cemetery, the victims being shot in batches of fifteen or twenty. Due to the youthful inaccuracy of the firing squad, few if any were killed at the first volley.

Similar massacres took place at Lyons, these being arranged by Representative Javogue. One took place on 8 February 1794 when twenty-eight victims were shot. They were led, tied together by a single rope, first to the scaffold where, in front of the guillotine, the death sentence was pronounced. From there they were paraded through the streets, the noise of their shuffling feet accompanied by a band playing the fifty-first psalm, 'Have mercy upon me, O God'.

On reaching an avenue of sycamores, the extremities of the rope were tied to two of the trees, thereby positioning the line of victims along the edge of a specially prepared deep ditch. They had to wait until Javogue arrived in his carriage, there to exult over the spectacle as, the order to fire being given, the dead and wounded collapsed into the trench. It is to the credit of the local republican soldiers that they took no part in the slaughter, the Representative having to arm some Piedmontese prisoners for the purpose. The volley was the signal for the poor of Lyons to scramble down into the trench, to strip the corpses of their clothes and valuables.

Henry Jephson, in his book *The Real French Revolutionist* written in 1899, tells of:

> an eye witness who was a twelve year old boy, and as curious and callous as boys of all countries are at that age. He was at the edge of the trench into which the bodies were being piled and he said that what impressed him most in that barbarous drama was not so much the sight of those tragic deaths, as the appearance of the bodies heaped in the common trench, curved one over the other, and seeming to shudder every time that another corpse was thrown on to the palpitating flesh.

A chapel of remembrance was later built nearby, in memory of those so brutally murdered that day.

Horror by gunfire differs little from horror inflicted by the guillotine, sword or wheel, it seems, and sheer bestiality lurks only fractionally below the veneer of so-called civilized societies. In this century however, judicial executions of civilians by firing squad are carried out in a rather more merciful manner. A good example is the comparatively recent case involving the American murderer Gary Marks Gilmore who, after serving over ten years' imprisonment for previous crimes, was released, only to gun down two defenceless men. This merciless killer would not have rated more than a line or two in American newspapers were it not for the fact that rather than face many more years in prison, Gilmore accepted the death sentence, elected to die by firing squad, and refused to appeal for a reprieve.

As subsequent months passed, the public's appetite for drama was repeatedly whetted as various bodies sought to appeal on his behalf – his mother, his lawyers, even the

State of Utah wherein he was imprisoned. Eventually all due processes of the law were exhausted, and Gilmore got his wish.

At sunrise on 19 January 1977 he was led to the execution shed. Under bright overhead lights at one end of the shed a chair had been positioned, banked on three sides by sandbags. Gilmore was strapped into the chair while a crowd of spectators, officials and reporters watched from one side. In the darkness at the far end of the shed the firing squad waited for the priest to complete his prayers for the condemned man. As he did so, a guard stepped forward, to place a black hood over Gilmore's head, and pin a circle of cloth over his heart, the white ring on a black background providing the aiming point for the men lined up in the shadows, their rifles at the ready.

As the guard withdrew, the signal was given, and the watchers scarcely had time to brace themselves before the deafening salvo of shots rang out, the crescendo of sound reverberating within the confines of the building. As the body slumped in the chair, the prison doctor advanced and confirmed that Gilmore's wish had at long last been granted, and justice had been done.

7 Macabre Miscellany

Considering that the human body is so vulnerable, having only one heart to pierce, one windpipe to squeeze, one brain to cleave, life should therefore be very easy to extinguish. Despite that, it is little short of amazing that so many countries should go to such great lengths in devising different ways of achieving the goal.

Methods of execution even varied with the crime, England in the 16th century sentencing common criminals to be hanged and heretics to be burned at the stake. This latter fate was deemed more appropriate for dissenters since it was considered that only flames could cleanse their defiled souls, and in London it took place at Smithfield, outside St Bartholomew's Hospital.

Over the years the flames claimed the lives of at least fifty-three men and eleven women, one victim being John Rogers, vicar of St Sepulchre's Church, Newgate. He had been sentenced to death on the orders of Queen Mary for preaching forbidden sermons outside St Paul's Church, and on 4 February 1555 his journey from Newgate Prison to Smithfield took him past his own church of St Sepulchre's where, according to Foxe's *Book of Martyrs*, 'his wife and children, eleven in number, ten able to go and one at the breast, met him as he passed'.

Arriving at Smithfield he was tied to a stake, probably by the hangman Stumpleg, and the faggots were ignited. It is not known whether he was granted the merciful privilege sometimes conceded to martyrs, of having a small bag of gunpowder hung around his neck in order to speed his demise and so reduce his suffering but, like the others, he died bravely.

In March 1849, during excavations to instal new sewers at Smithfield, the workmen's spades uncovered a mass of rough stones three feet below the surface. These boulders were blackened as if by fire and were encrusted with ash. Charred human bones, partially consumed by the flames, lay among the stones and these remains were taken away, revered as holy relics.

It was inevitable that the progress of science, namely the discovery of electricity, would permit a more sophisticated, if not more humane, method of execution, and it is only fitting that one of the more innovative nations in the world, the United States of America, should have utilized that discovery to dispatch some of their criminals.

It is also somewhat significant that the Americans, always lovers of comfort, should opt for a method involving a chair. To receive the axe one kneels submissively, for hanging one stands on tremulous legs; face down with neck pinioned, on the guillotine, and on one's back, sacrificial-style, on the wheel. If nothing else, the American method of sitting in a chair, albeit one connected to the mains, is a basically civilized posture in which to depart this life.

'Old Smokey' or the 'Hot Squat' as the electric chair became colloquially known, replaced hanging in the State of New York, being adopted by Governor David B. Hill on 4 June 1888. During the next twelve years Ohio, Massachusetts, New Jersey, Virginia and North Carolina followed suit enthusiastically, over a hundred electrocutions taking place by 1906.

The layout inside gaols so equipped was basically the same. In each, the area assigned to those condemned to death was virtually a prison within a prison, having its own exercise yard, kitchen and small hospital, with separate cell blocks for men and women prisoners.

A typical newspaper report of the 1930s described how, early in the morning of his execution, the prisoner was transferred to a pre-execution cell in a corridor incorporating the execution room and the morgue, and at the appointed time warders entered the cell. One of them would slit open the prisoner's right trouser leg. They, and the chaplain, then escorted him into the execution chamber where a number of officials and reporters sat opposite the electric chair, a heavy, high-backed piece of furniture made of oak, fitted with straps to enable the warders to secure the prisoner's arms and legs, head and chest.

An electrode, moistened with salt solution to ensure a good contact, was next attached to the prisoner's head, and another to the now bare flesh of his right leg. After a black hood had been dropped over the prisoner's head, the prison warden checked the contacts, straps and hood, and gave the signal. A few feet away, behind the chair, the executioner operated the switch on an instrument panel, sending a lethal current of 1,800–2,000 volts, 5 amps, coursing through the victim's body for about five seconds, the charge emitting a droning hum through the room. After being reduced to 500 volts, it was increased twice more, three such charges inevitably proving fatal. After being certified dead by the prison doctor, the body was then removed for an autopsy and subsequent burial.

The first man to die in that fashion was William Kemmler, a jealous husband who had murdered his wife. On 6 August 1890 he was strapped into the chair in Auburn State prison and there paid the penalty.

Some years later, in 1895, the *New York World* printed a story exposing a Doctor Buchanan who, in order to finance his gambling, insured and then murdered his wife. A factor widely discussed in the medical journals of the day was an allegation that he had killed his wife with morphine and had destroyed the evidence of this method by putting belladonna into her eyes to dilate the pinpoint pupils. As proof, an inoffensive cat was put to death in the courtroom, to prove the doctor's guilt. The jury were evidently convinced, and he died in the Sing Sing electric chair later in the year.

That particular prison is probably as well known in Britain as in the States. Portrayed in films and books for decades, its harsh, sometimes brutal reputation seems to epitomize the archetypal American prison. Yet in the 1920s the living conditions of its inmates were radically improved, with the appointment of Mr Lewis Lawes as warden. This wise and humane administrator served in office for over twelve years and was responsible not only for the well-being and control of its thousands of prisoners but also for the executions of 150 men and one woman during those years.

The woman was Ruth May Snyder, who was so cold-blooded a killer that she earned the nickname of the 'Granite Woman'. Down the ages other women have been just as murderous, but Ruth Snyder received international publicity when her picture appeared in newspapers all over the world, a picture secretly taken of her at the very moment of her electrocution.

She had been sentenced to death for the murder of her husband, whom she had previously insured for nearly $100,000. Together with her lover Judd Gray, she had battered her husband with a lead sash weight, doped him with chloroform and finished him off by strangling him with picture wire.

In Sing Sing's condemned cells both wrote their autobiographies, these being eagerly sought by the press whose representatives besieged the prison night and day. While the appeals for commutation of the death sentences were being heard, Ruth received over 150 proposals of marriage and, refusing to accept the inevitable outcome of her callous deed, hoped for a reprieve.

But it was not to be. The day before her execution, 11 January 1928, she lapsed into a trance-like state, but in the evening revived sufficiently to have her hair done by the wardress guarding her. Overnight the crowds had been massing in their hundreds outside the prison gates, growing quiet as the time approached. Inside the condemned block Ruth was led to the electric chair. The straps were secured, the contacts attached to her body. To screen her from the scores of witnesses, her wardress had been detailed to stand in front of her but, overwhelmed no doubt by the ordeal of having to look at a woman about to die, she collapsed and had to be carried out. And as the executioner switched on the current, so a reporter seized the opportunity to operate the hidden camera strapped to his ankle. Blurred and indistinct, the photograph left everything to the imagination, but became a historic scoop.

Another event that attracted international headlines a little earlier was Colonel Charles Lindbergh's record-breaking solo flight across the Atlantic in 1927. Five years later the world was stunned and horrified at the kidnapping of Lindbergh's baby son for a large ransom.

In May 1932 the baby's body was found buried in the vicinity of the house and the search for the ruthless killer was intensified. Such was the publicity that a garage attendant, checking his takings against the list of currency numbers issued by the police, found one that matched. The driver, identified by his car registration number, was Bruno Hauptmann, a former German soldier.

Further evidence was immediately forthcoming when a search of his house revealed a large part of the ransom money. Despite his protestations of innocence, he was electrocuted in Trenton State Prison, New Jersey, in April 1936.

Not all criminals were overwhelmed by the solemnity of the occasion however. When George Appel, a Chicago gangster, was being strapped in the electric chair, he gave the watching press men his quote-worthy final words: 'Well folks, you'll soon see a baked Appel!'

But, as in any other method of execution, mishaps also occurred, and it must have been horrific when, at Auburn Prison in 1893, the back of the chair broke just as the victim William Taylor was lapsing into unconsciousness. The current was switched off and the officials quickly removed Taylor to a nearby cell where he was kept insensible by drugs while repairs took place. An hour later he was carried to the chair and duly paid the price for his crime.

This seemingly callous treatment was in fact compassionate, for the victim could have known nothing after first lapsing into insensibility, and so died without further suffering.

Regrettably, due no doubt to official regulations, the identities of the Electrical Lords of the Scaffold were rarely published, probably for the same reasons that induced their medieval counterparts to disguise themselves with masks and false beards. But there was never any shortage of volunteers for the post, any vacancy attracting hundreds of applications.

Although the anonymity of the executioner was preserved, the crimes of their more notorious victims were given worldwide publicity. One was Albert Fish who, not content with murder, indulged in cannibalism as well, to satisfy his perverted tastes. Masochistically he inserted needles into his own flesh and although his defence lawyer sought to declare him not responsible for his own actions the jury thought otherwise. In January 1936 at Sing Sing Prison he was hooded and strapped in the chair. The first attempt at electrocution failed, some reporters attributing this to the number of needles still in Fish's body, but a second charge proved successful.

The electric chairs in the various states were widely used, over 3,800 executions being carried out between 1930 and 1972. Not all were those of murderers. One at least was a would-be assassin who attempted to kill the president elect of the United States, Franklin Delano Roosevelt.

Guiseppe Zangara had a grudge against all capitalists, kings, heads of state and members of the privileged classes. A loner, he nurtured his grievances for years until, in 1931, he resolved to kill Roosevelt.

In Miami, at a large public meeting addressed by the president to be, Zangara saw and seized his opportunity, emptying his revolver at his unsuspecting human target. According to subsequent newspaper reports, Roosevelt escaped unscathed because of various bystanders who claimed to have deflected Zangara's aim by one means or another. Others in the presidential party were not so fortunate, the mayor of Miami dying from gunshot wounds, and some spectators were injured, though none fatally. One wonders, not without apprehensive hindsight, how the death of Roosevelt would have affected the outcome of the Second World War, in which he was such a staunch and supportive ally of Great Britain.

Zangara pleaded guilty at his trial, maintaining his contempt for society even as he was escorted into the death cell. Without waiting to be led to the chair, arrogantly he strode across and sat down in it, to be hooded and bound. Defiant to the end, he continued his protests as the switch sent the first charge through him. After his death his body, as in English executions, was buried in an anonymous grave behind the prison walls.

Another assassin, a more accurate and deadly marksman, was Leon Czolgosz. Anarchistic in his principles, he was pathologically opposed to any form of government or any one person wielding power. And when, on 6 September 1901, President McKinley attended a public reception at the Pan-American Exposition in Buffalo, Czolgosz took his place patiently in the long queue of people formed up to shake the President's hand.

As more recent assassination attempts have shown, it is virtually impossible to guarantee one hundred per cent protection for any public figure, even with the resources of modern technology. And so, despite there being scores of police and soldiers in the hall, the inconspicuous figure of Czolgosz attracted little attention other than his having a bandaged right hand. And as the President reached out yet again, this time to shake hands with Czolgosz, the assassin fired through the handkerchief which concealed his gun. Both bullets hit the President, wounding him so severely that he died a week later. The cold-blooded murderer was brought to trial, although he refused to recognize the court or its authority.

On 29 October 1901, still loudly justifying his actions in ridding the people of an enemy, he was strapped into the electric chair at Auburn State Prison. The switch was operated and after death had been certified by the doctors, the body was placed in a coffin. Before being buried, sulphuric acid was poured over the body, obliterating every trace of the assassin's existence.

Most executions were well attended by members of the press, who would later go into lurid details of the victim's reactions, recounting the spasmodic convulsions of the body, the violent tensing of the neck muscles, the wisps of smoke rising from beneath the hood. But whether such initial paroxysms are conscious efforts to resist the shock of the current, or just muscular contractions after death, is open to question.

The latter premise is supported by some medical authorities who point out that the death-dealing effect on the vital organs occurs infinitely faster than the pain caused can travel through the nerve fibres to the brain. So it could well be that the victim was already dead by the time the witnesses recoiled in horror, and to anyone who has experienced even a mild shock, it must certainly seem that a powerful one would indeed kill instantly.

Yet oddly enough, experiments utilizing electricity were in the past used, not to execute the living, but seemingly to revive the dead! On 13 January 1803 murderer George Foster was hanged in London and his body handed over for dissection. In the hospital Professor Aldini decided to assess the effects of passing an electric current through the corpse, the galvanic process as it was called.

The results were remarkable, for those present saw the cadaver's mouth moving, its face twitching. One eye actually opened and the legs started to move. This Frankenstein-like spectacle so traumatized some of the onlookers that one, Mr Pass, the beadle of the Barber Surgeon Company, went home and died from a heart attack.

The electric chair is still in use in Georgia, Louisiana, Arkansas and Florida, though some disquiet has recently been voiced regarding the serviceability of the one used in Florida's State Prison at Starke. Journalists present at the execution of murderer Jesse Tafero early in 1990 reported sparks coming from the chair itself, whilst smoke and a smell of burning flesh filled the chamber, although the authorities claimed that nevertheless the victim had died instantly.

Another judicial method of execution adopted in the United States was the gas chamber, a method which also involved the use of a chair. This was introduced in 1924 in the State of Nevada, to replace more barbaric forms of execution. Whether it turned out to be just as barbaric is open to conjecture.

As its name implies, the gas chamber is a small airtight room made of steel, with a plate glass observation window, containing one or more chairs bolted to the floor. The victim is strapped into a chair, near to which is positioned a container of sulphuric acid.

After the room has been vacated by the officials and the signal given, the executioner in the adjoining control room pulls a red-painted lever. This turns a rod extending into the gas chamber, allowing it to lower a cloth sachet of sodium cyanide pellets into the acid. The chemical reaction so generated gives off hydrogen cyanide (HCN), prussic acid.

Exposure to 300 parts of this lethal cocktail per one million parts of air is rapidly fatal, almost instantaneous death from asphyxiation resulting, if the victim breathes deeply. As with most 'instantaneous' methods of execution, it does not always pay to believe the advertisements.

In the same way as the electric chair became popular with some states, so others adopted the gas-chamber method, one being installed in San Quentin Prison, California. In the 1930s San Francisco newspapers, the *Examiner*, the *Chronicle* and others, devoted many paragraphs to this latest innovation, especially when the city authorities tested the apparatus on live pigs. Many of the reporters who attended, hoping for some good copy, were repelled by what they saw, some describing it as more savage than being hanged, drawn and quartered.

Nor did their editors modify their opinions when, in 1938, they printed their accounts of two murderers who were gassed, the grisly descriptions including the fact that nearly fifteen minutes elapsed before death was confirmed. American newspaper and magazine reporters were permitted to attend executions as a matter of course, and few failed to describe the scene in detail when Barbara Graham met her death in San Quentin's gas chamber in 1955. But perhaps the case which attracted the most international interest was that of Caryl Chessman, the 'Red Light Bandit'. Every aspect of his trial, the long drawn-out appeals and lengthy imprisonment on San Quentin Death Row was covered in full, right up to the day in 1960 when he was finally escorted to the gas chamber.

More than fifty representatives of the press were present, and even the most hardened hack must have been shocked at the sight of the victim's convulsive reactions as the gas took effect. The fact that such victims are not hooded, because such a covering would provide a pocket of air, meant that Chessman's every facial distortion was visible, and nearly ten minutes elapsed before the doctor pronounced him dead. This confirmation was made possible by means of a long stethoscope tube, a diaphragm at one end having been attached to the victim's chest when strapped into the chair, and the tube extending through the chamber wall so that the heartbeats could be monitored.

Only then was a fan switched on, to expel the poisonous fumes through a tall chimney, before prison officials, led by the warden responsible for the execution, Mr F. R. Dickson, entered, to have Chessman's body removed for burial.

San Quentin's gas chamber, unused since 1967, is inspected every three months, its equipment tested with as much thoroughness as is England's gallows. Until 1985 Mr Joseph Ferritti, a gas-chamber warder, was one of the acknowledged experts on its operation, having been present at 126 executions, but with his retirement and a crowded Death Row, a new generation of executioners will soon be required.

Before the gas chamber and electric chair, the traditional method introduced into the country by the early English settlers, that of hanging, was employed. Unlike the old English penal code, however, under which those guilty of high treason were disembowelled while still alive, Americans who killed their presidents were spared such mutilation.

One such case occurred in 1881 when the assassination of President Garfield stunned the nation. The culprit was Charles Guiteau, an evangelist who, after earlier studying law, became obsessed by ambitions of gaining political power and prestige. By supporting the President, he reasoned, he could persuade Garfield to make him at least a consul, preferably an ambassador, and that would later lead on to the White House itself, and the office of president.

Pursuing his grandiose fantasies, he bombarded Garfield and his aides with letters, putting himself forward for various political appointments. Understandably classed as a public nuisance and a crank, he grew resentful and, having convinced himself that the President was betraying the Republican Party with the wrong policies, decided to kill him.

On 2 July 1881 President Garfield arrived at the Washington railway station *en route* to New Jersey. As he entered the waiting room Guiteau walked up behind him and shot him in the back, mortally wounding him. Despite continued and desperate efforts by the doctors over the following weeks, the President died two months later.

The trial of Guiteau lasted more than twelve weeks and became a social gathering. Everyone who was anyone attended, newspapers sending not only their crime reporters, but their fashion editors as well, to do justice to the scene, if not to the accused man. Guiteau's own behaviour contributed to the general mêlée. Day after day his irrational outbursts made the headlines, but the highlight of the trial occurred when the very section of the late President's spine which had been hit by Guiteau's bullet was produced in evidence and passed around the courtroom, surely one of the most bizarre exhibits of all time.

The assassin was found guilty and was sentenced to be hanged. Eccentric to the end, he left a note bequeathing his body to the chaplain, adding the proviso that it should not be used for any commercial purpose.

On 30 June 1882, amid scenes reminiscent of those at Tyburn centuries before, Charles Guiteau was taken to the execution room and positioned on the drop. Outside the gaol a 5,000-strong crowd had gathered, whiling away the time by singing and joking, sustained by the refreshments on sale. And, as reported by the *Washington Evening Star*, tickets at $300 each had changed hands in order that some 250 spectators could watch the hooded and noosed figure drop through the trap and so be able to tell their grandchildren that they had seen the execution of the man who killed the president.

There was also a good attendance a little later that century when, in 1898, justice caught up with the 'Demon Killer of the Belfry'. This melodramatic title was bestowed by the American press, who had a field day when Theodore Durrant murdered two young women in a San Francisco church.

Every detail of the hanging was recounted by the scores of reporters among the 150 spectators in San Quentin's execution chamber, a crowd which included Durrant's father. The killer's mother waited in an adjoining room, the parents' morbid eccentricity showing itself in their wish to have the execution filmed, a request that was rejected.

The funereal procession entered the large room, presided over by the prison's Lord of the Scaffold Amos Lunt who, after the appropriate prayers had been said, positioned the victim on the trap. Hangman may have been his title, but oddly enough he was not the one who released the trap. For on a signal given by the warden, each of three warders standing behind a nearby screen severed a rope, only one of which operated the trap-release mechanism.

This arrangement neatly absolved the feeling of personal blame and responsibility experienced by the men, in the same way as firing squad members felt consoled by the knowledge that some rifles had blank ammunition. And the crowds whose hands pulled on the rope of the Halifax gibbet centuries earlier must have felt the same. Society in general firmly believes that wrongdoers should be punished, as long as they themselves don't have to press the button or swing the axe.

After Durrant's execution the body was placed in a coffin and taken into the next room, where the parents grieved over their dead son. However, the Californian newspapers made much of the fact that Mr and Mrs Durrant rapidly got over their trauma and, sitting by the coffin, partook of a hearty meal, one paper claiming that Mrs Durrant asked for a further helping of roast beef!

Needless to say, the public's fascination with the affair was exploited to the full by the more unscrupulous, the hanging rope being sold at a dollar an inch.

Another early colony which adopted hanging was Hong Kong. One of its recent hangmen was the efficient and dedicated John Fleming, who deftly dispatched his hooded and strait-jacketed victims for the princely sum of seventy-five Hong Kong dollars each.

On the mainland of China, capital punishment through the ages assumed many excruciating forms. Under Manchu law, victims could be flogged by 'lictors' wielding long, thin bamboo canes. So adept were they that they could strike hundreds of times without blistering the skin, or could draw blood with three blows. If the court decreed extra severity, the lictors would flick the bamboo so that it tore off flesh in strips.

Such expertise was achieved only by constant practice on a block of bean curd, a substance resembling thick custard, perfection not being reached until they were able to strike repeatedly without breaking the surface.

As in England, where it was considered indecent to expose a woman in order that she could be drawn and quartered, so in China women's modesty was equally respected. They were allowed to retain their lower garments but were punished by being caned on their mouths or hands, or by having their breasts pierced by hot irons.

China's ancient civilization has often been given the credit for being inventive, so it is hardly surprising that the guillotine is said to have originated there, albeit in a primitive form. It consisted of a tree trunk, ten feet in length, one end being hinged to a horizontal beam by means of a strong bronze pin, a large triangular blade being fixed to the other end. The trunk was propped up vertically by a loose support, and the victim tied to pegs in the ground. The prop was then knocked away, allowing the trunk to fall with devastating force, its blade severing the head instantaneously.

Mexico found the firing squad highly effective, as did Thailand, though the Thai 'squad' consisted, at least until 1984, of just one man! He was Pathom Kruapeng, a Lord of the Scaffold who, in his fourteen years of service, executed fifty criminals.

As a devout Buddhist he followed a strict ritual on the day of execution, in which he asked the victim for forgiveness by raising a stone and a yellow flower in the air. Not that Pathom could see the condemned man who, hidden behind a cloth screen, was strapped into a chair, with his back to the screen. The victim's arms were secured to a long pole, and in his hands he held symbolic joss sticks and flowers.

Pathom, some twenty-five feet away, stationed himself at an automatic rifle fixed to a stand, its sights trained on a target marked on the screen. When a red flag was lowered, Pathom fired the rifle, continuing until being signalled that the victim was dead. Up to five shots were sometimes needed, and Pathom received the equivalent of nearly £40 for each execution.

This unusual form of capital punishment, involving just one man firing at an unseen target, was made even more extraordinary by the fact that the identity of the victim was not revealed to the executioner until the following day.

No religious ceremony, no anonymity, accompanied the executions on Christmas Day 1989 when President Nicolae Ceauşescu and his wife Elena paid the price following revolution in Romania. After interrogation by a military court they were taken to an adjoining area and shot, the firing squad consisting of one officer and two soldiers with machine guns. It was subsequently reported that the soldiers opened fire before being ordered, emptying their magazines and aiming so wildly that others present received bullet wounds.

Europe generally tended to employ more traditional devices than guns, Holland's murderers being broken on the wheel as recently as 1805. Neighbouring Belgium also

used the wheel earlier in its history, one victim pleading to
remain modestly clad while undergoing execution.
Accordingly she mounted the scaffold wearing a white
satin jacket and pantaloons.

More recently Belgium adopted the guillotine, and the
author inspected one in Liège in the 1970s. Although it
was apparently in full working order, capital punishment
is no longer in force in that country.

Conclusion

So the scaffold reaps its harvest and the long cavalcade files past. Men and women, with heads twisted awry from the rope or with limbs shattered on the wheel, scourged by the knout or headless from the blade. Some are seared by the flames or riddled by bullets, others mutilated by knives or poisoned by the gas chamber.

But do not waste undue sympathy on those who were the murderers or terrorists of their day; visualize instead the even longer procession of those whom *they* had maimed and slaughtered, the innocent victims whose sufferings are overlooked when the punishment awarded to their attackers is deplored and condemned as excessive.

If society decrees that the law of the land should include capital punishment, by whatever means, as an integral part of its system of justice, then it should continue to praise its efficient police for detecting the criminals, reward its skilful lawyers for prosecuting them, and ennoble its impartial judges for sentencing them.

But without one essential profession, all those officers of the law would be merely cardboard cut-outs, obtaining their salaries under false pretences. So just for once, let us all applaud:

The Lords of the Scaffold!

Select Bibliography

Andrews, W., *Old Time Punishments* (Andrews & Co, 1890)

Andrews, W., *England in Days of Old* (Andrews & Co, 1897)

Bayley, J., *History of the Tower* (T. Cadell, 1825)

Bell, D., *Chapel in the Tower* (Murray, 1877)

Davey, R., *The Tower of London* (Methuen, 1910)

Dixon, H., *Her Majesty's Tower*, (Bickers & Son, 1885)

Evelyn, J., *Diary of John Evelyn*, (Bickers & Bush, 1879)

Gallioni, A., *Tortures & Torments of the Christian Martyrs* (Fortuna Press, 1903)

Gerard, J., *The Condition of Catholics under James I* (edited by Fr. Morris, 1871)

Gregory, W., *Gregory's Chronicles* (Camden, 1876)

Hall, E., *Hall's Chronicles* (1809 edition)

Harper, C.G., *Half Hours with the Highwaymen* (Chapman & Hall, 1908)

Holinshed, R., *Holinshed's Chronicles* (edited by J. Hooker, 1586)

Howard, J., *State of the Prisons* (Eyres, 1777)

Jephson, H., *The Real French Revolutionist* (Macmillan, 1899)

Johnson, T., *A Gossiping Book about Lancaster Castle* (1893)

Lenotre, G., *The Guillotine and its Servants* (Hutchinson, 1908)

Lowrie, D., *My Life in Prison* (Lane, 1912)

Macauley, T.B., *Lord Macauley's History of England* (1866)

Machyn, T., *Diary of a London Resident* (Camden, 1848)

Marks, A., *Tyburn Tree, its History and Annals* (Brown, Langham, 1908)

Nutt, D., *Folklore of Yorkshire* (1901)

Sanson, H., *Memoirs of the Sanson Family 1688–1847*, (Chatto & Windus, 1876)

Schmidt, F., *Hangman's Diary* (Philip Allan & Co, 1928)

Scott, J., *Bygone Cumberland and Westmorland* (1899)

Stow, J., *London under Elizabeth* (Routledge & Sons, 1890)

Tasker, R.J., *Grimhaven* (Knopf, 1928)

Thornbury, R., *Old & New London*, (Cassell, Petter & Galpin 1893/4)

Timbs, J., *Romance of London* (Frederick Warne, 1865)

Williamson, A., *General Williamson's Diary*, (Camden, 1912)

Calendar of State Papers (Domestic Series)

Chronicles of Crime (Camden Pelham, 1887)

Gentleman's Magazine (1750, 1829)

Middlesex Session Rolls

Newgate Calendar (Miles & Co, 1891)

Notable British Trials series

Yorkshire Notes and Queries (Derwent, 1905)

Tower of London records

Tyburn Gallows (London County Council, 1909)

Index

Index

A selection of bestsellers from Headline

FICTION

DANCING ON THE RAINBOW	Frances Brown	£4.99 ☐
NEVER PICK UP HITCH-HIKERS!	Ellis Peters	£4.50 ☐
THE WOMEN'S CLUB	Margaret Bard	£5.99 ☐
A WOMAN SCORNED	M. R. O'Donnell	£4.99 ☐
THE FALL OF HYPERION	Dan Simmons	£5.99 ☐
SIRO	David Ignatius	£4.99 ☐
DARKNESS, TELL US	Richard Laymon	£4.99 ☐
THE BOTTOM LINE	John Harman	£5.99 ☐

NON-FICTION

ROD STEWART	Tim Ewbank & Stafford Hildred	£4.99 ☐
JOHN MAJOR	Bruce Anderson	£6.99 ☐
WHITE HEAT	Marco Pierre White	£5.99 ☐

SCIENCE FICTION AND FANTASY

LENS OF THE WORLD	R. A. MacAvoy	£4.50 ☐
DREAM FINDER	Roger Taylor	£5.99 ☐
VENGEANCE FOR A LONELY MAN	Simon R. Green	£4.50 ☐

All Headline books are available at your local bookshop or newsagent, or can be ordered direct from the publisher. Just tick the titles you want and fill in the form below. Prices and availability subject to change without notice.

Headline Book Publishing PLC, Cash Sales Department, PO Box 11, Falmouth, Cornwall, TR10 9EN, England.

Please enclose a cheque or postal order to the value of the cover price and allow the following for postage and packing:
UK & BFPO: £1.00 for the first book, 50p for the second book and 30p for each additional book ordered up to a maximum charge of £3.00.
OVERSEAS & EIRE: £2.00 for the first book, £1.00 for the second book and 50p for each additional book.

Name ....

Address ....

....

....